# JOHN MARK LOUSE
## *a light to Karamoja*

Foreword
by
JAMES M. VEREMU

Introduction
by
ISAAC WONYIMA

Farewell
by
ANDREW C. PHIRI

Epilogue & Testimony
by
RICHARD GAN

Compiled, edited, and published by
ANDREW C. PHIRI
*Reflections* on *Faith*
voiceoftheword@live.com | www.andrewcphiri.com

ISBN 978-9982-9986-9-7

This book is made available to you with prayer that the testimonies and sermons contained herein may draw you closer to Christ in this late hour.

Believers' Assembly
PO Box 37919
Lusaka
Republic of Zambia

NOTE: We often receive many requests for books. Kindly be informed that due to many demands of ministry work we can only afford to send free copies when resources are available. You can help us cover printing and shipment expenses by buying yourself a copy direct from Amazon.com. Otherwise send your request to:

bookrequest@andrewcphiri.com

**John Mark Louse**
**(1955-2015)**

…Then something happened. I heard on the outside of the hut a mighty rocking and blowing wind. It was shaking the hut and was even tearing into the hut. This wind first put out the cigarette, then later the *"tad hoper"* and the hut became dark but the wind persisted. There was a quaking of the earth. With such persistent blowing wind and a darkened room, my strength went off and I became paralyzed. Suddenly a light appeared in the hut and immediately the wind and the quaking stopped. The nature of this light was unique; it had a bluish brightness. All these happenings were too much for me, and I wanted to run away but I got paralyzed…

# Contents


Foreword     8

Introduction     10

I.   Call to the Ministry     14

II.   Testimonies of Believers     33

III.   Transcribed sermons

    *Simeon*     44

    *Way of Escape*     71

    *Wondrous Things*     96

Farewell     122

Epilogue     126

# *Foreword*

I had heard about Brother John Mark and how God had called and used him. It was in the year of our Lord 1998 when 1 was attending a convention in Eldoret Kenya that 1 first met him.

We shared adjacent rooms at the school dormitory where we were lodging but I could not distinguish him. Someone asked me "Have you met Brother John Mark?" I said "No, where is he?" The person told me that he was just next to my room and that is when I met him.

You couldn't tell from looks who he was. I saw this tall slim and very ordinary humble soft spoken man. After this I visited the areas where he had pioneered the Gospel of Salvation in Uganda and saw the great impact of the Word of God in the very backward regions of Karamoja, in the northern part of the country. The testimony of his calling was painted before me in plain view.

This is John Mark Louse who was called to be an apostle. On three occasions he visited my country. On the first trip I was privileged to take him on a tour of Zambia and Malawi. Here I witnessed the wonderful gift of apostleship in operation in the humble ministry. On the third and final trip to Zimbabwe towards the end of the year 2015 Brother John Mark ministered in our church and some others who desired his return. But the Lord did not permit it for he was called home on 26th February 2015.

But this last trip which to us was his farewell to the brethren was most outstanding. His itinerary started with Zambia. From there he came here in Zimbabwe after which he returned to Zambia for some more services. From Zambia he went to Tanzania and Kenya. It was a trip of going round in various places as if to say goodbye to the saints. The places he had visited in Zimbabwe wanted him to visit again but it wasn't  long after his return home in Uganda that the Lord took him.

I was privileged to preach at his funeral. Although he left to be with the Lord, his influence and legacy was not interred with his bones. It will live long in our memory, as a witness, that an Apostle came our way.

James M. Veremu
*Zimbabwe*

# *Introduction*

Pastor John Mark Louse hails from Mogos Village in Matheniko County of Moroto district in Karamoja Region. Karamoja is situated in the north-eastern part of Uganda (see map below). The natives of Karamoja are called Karamojongs and so John Mark is a Karamojong.

Karamojongs are nomadic pastoralists. They are primitive and are renowned for moving about naked. Their livelihood depends on cattle and limited cultivation of crops, especially sorghum that is often used for brew during festivals such as marriage and certain other rituals.

Karamojongs are also known for their ritualistic sacrifice of humans which they believe prevents disasters like wars and diseases when diviners tell them of such misfortune befalling the land.

Karamoja is a region that has numerous ethnic tribes such as Matheniko, Bokora, Pian, Tepes, and Jie, Dodoth and Labwor. All these tribes often fight each other for cattle.

Karamojongs are known to be the most unlearned tribe in Uganda. Because of their backwardness, ignorance and poverty, they often go on rampage in cattle rustling amongst themselves and other surrounding neighbouring districts such as Teso, Lango, Acholi and Kapchorwa.

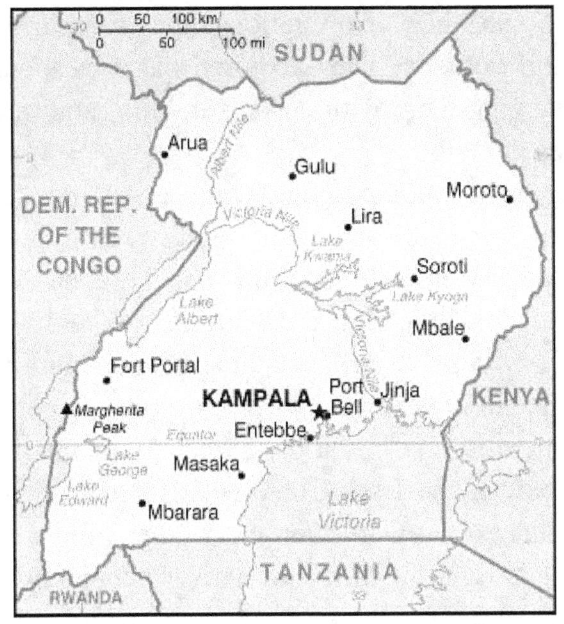


*Map of Uganda*

Karamojongs generally used spears, bows and arrows to fight. However, when Idi Amin's government was overthrown in 1979, the warriors raided the Moroto Army Barracks. They took the guns, tied them up in bundles as one tied up firewood gathered in the bush. Thus, guns and ammunitions are aplenty in the area. This act of lawlessness persisted till the NRM (National Resistance Movement), under the leadership of His Excellency Yoweri Kaguta Museveni, came into power in 1986. From that time the Karamojongs began to get their ammunitions and guns from Sudan and Somalia. They acquired these weapons by exchanging them with cows, sorghum, and in a few cases money.

Being armed, Karamojong pose serious danger and harm to people in neighbouring regions and that includes Kenyans, especially the Turkana and Pokot people. They would waylay people and rob them. They also used guns against government forces that are in the area.

Karamoja is certainly a dark world, perhaps the darkest part of the Dark Continent! However, it is in such places that God often works the wonder of causing His light to shine and deliver people from forces of darkness. Thankfully, this is exactly what happened in Karamoja!

Find in this book an amazing story of one, John Mark Louse, a karamojong warrior who experienced a miraculous visitation of the Lord Jesus Christ and was given an apostolic ministry to become a mighty warrior of faith and a light to his people. Many of us are eye witnesses of the great work God wrought through his ministry and can testify in the words of Isaiah saying, *"people that walked in darkness have seen a great light: they that dwell in the land of the shadow of death, upon them hath the light shined"* (Isa.9:2).

Find in this book, first, an intriguing testimony

of the call of John Mark, second, three transcribed sermons he preached during his visit to Zambia, and third, miscellaneous testimonies which we hope will stir your faith to walk closely with the Lord in this late hour.

Isaac Wonyima
*Uganda*

# I
# CALL TO THE MINISTRY

The Karamojongs being primitive and uneducated, it is not surprising that I, Pastor John Mark Louse, am also uneducated. I did not attend any formal education in my lifetime.

When I was about 7 years old (back in the 1960s), I had worries about the prevalence of death in the region. One day I thought to myself, "Is there no way how one can be saved from death?" In the night the angel of the Lord visited me and told me, "In the near future, you will go to a land; you will be directed to a land where people cannot die."

As I grew up, I was put to shepherd the cattle of my father and when the Turkana people (from Kenya) attacked the kraals and raided the cattle, I narrowly survived death. Given the fact that all the cattle were taken, I had no work at home since the only thing for my livelihood had been taken away. I went to stay in Moroto town in search of a way to survive. But faced with the challenge of having to sleep on people's verandas and other unbearable challenges, such as facing hunger, I decided to go to Teso.

The hardships in Moroto town drove me to talk to a fellow wanderer, who was a friend, about fleeing to Teso District. The year was 1969. We went to Teso and on arrival at Soroti town we stayed together with other Karamojongs whom we found there as we searched for jobs for our survival.

One week after our arrival at Soroti, two men came looking for boys to take care of their cattle in their villages. One of them took me and the other my friend. That is how we parted.

On arrival at the home of the one who took me, I discovered that he was a Pentecostal believer, and he gave me the job of herding his cattle. The church people began ministering to me about salvation which I didn't know since I originally was a catholic. I told them that I had my religion so it is difficult to change to another religion. They persistently continued sharing with me the Word of God slowly, little by little, until 1970.

**They year I met the Lord**

One evening in the month of March in 1971 an extraordinary event happened. As usual, I took the cows home from the field, had supper and after having chatted with the other friends, went into my hut where I resided. I entered and sat down on my bed. I was a smoker then and had a lighted cigarette and was puffing away. Beside the bed was a "tad hoper" (a small container with fuel-paraffin and a wick for lighting). Then something happened. I heard on the outside of the hut a mighty rocking and blowing wind. It was shaking the hut and was even tearing into the hut. This wind first put out the cigarette, then later the "tad hoper" and the hut became dark but the wind persisted. There was a quaking of the earth. With such persistent blowing wind and a darkened room, my strength went off and I became paralyzed.

Suddenly a light appeared in the hut and immediately the wind and the quaking stopped. The nature of this light was unique; it had a bluish brightness. All these happenings were too much for me, and I wanted to run away but I got paralyzed. My joints were weakened; they refused to respond to my command to take off. My strength was gone.

In the light, the Lord Jesus Christ appeared. He looked directly at me with a lovely smiling face. He pointed at me and said, "My servant, you have been highly favoured. Your purpose of being here in Teso are for two reasons. You have been brought here because of salvation and secondly, you have a ministry; you are my Apostle and my appearing to you is to give you this ministry."

During this time, as the Lord was talking, I had a question deep inside my heart and the question was, "How will I preach the Word of God as an Apostle since I am not educated?" I did not utter it out. But the Lord again pointed at me and said, "I know why you doubt, I am going to give you the ability to understand English to minister my Word.

You will be able to speak, read and write for I have chosen you to be a light to your people. You are going to begin this ministry here in Teso, and you will continue with it even up to Karamoja and other lands. You will also fly in planes to other countries to minister my Word."

As Jesus was talking my strength came back slowly but surely and I became strong. Then He told me, "Go to Gideon's home (that is, the owner of the cows), to pray for you." (This man Gideon was the head of all the Pentecostals in Uganda). After talking to me for long, I was very happy and I felt a change inside me and my inner man was liberated. The Lord then disappeared together with the light.

I came out of the hut, locked the door and began the journey to Gideon's home which was about 300 metres from my hut. As I began walking, I looked up into the sky and I saw a great light in the form of a ball leading me to Gideon's home in the dark night. Arriving at Gideon's home, I knocked on the door and he opened, and without hesitation he questioned me, "It is now midnight, why are you here?" I answered him, "I have come here to be prayed for because Jesus appeared to me and told me to come and be prayed for." And believing that something had happened to me, the preacher prayed for me. I returned to my hut with happiness in my heart. Reaching my hut I slept and I had a dream that night. I saw in the dream heaven opened up and a man, looking like an angel, came down with what looked like a bucket containing what looked like oil. When he reached me he poured it out on me, upon my head down to the rest of my body.

When I woke up from the dream, I found myself kneeling and praying in other tongues by the bed. I kept praying for a long time. I wondered asking myself, "What is this that is happening to me?" I could not understand.

The next morning I took the cows out for grazing in the bush and at about 1:00pm when the cows were satisfied and gathered under a tree, I sat down under another tree. I pondered upon the events that took place that night and then a song came into my mind which says, "Oh the blood of Jesus" and I began singing that song. Right then another miraculous wonder took place. Fire fell on me and I saw flames all around me as though it was consuming the grass. There and then I entered into speaking in tongues again for a long time and a voice spoke to me and said, "You have been baptized with the Holy Ghost." When all was over I took the cows home.

At Pastor Gideon's home, after having supper as a family, they requested me to give a testimony of what things happened to me the previous night. I gave them the testimony including the one in the morning in the bush. They were very happy and said that I was blessed because God had also baptized me with the Holy Ghost. As we were about to enter into prayer I encouraged those who were not baptized with the Holy Spirit to believe that the Lord was able to baptize them also. As we prayed, the Lord baptized the family with the Holy Spirit, and amongst them was a demon possessed woman who got her deliverance.

When Sunday came, I requested the Pastor (though I didn't know how to read) to buy for me an Ateso Bible. (Ateso is one of Ugandan local languages). I gave him seven shillings and the following day he brought the Bible to me. Every time I go herding, I would carry the Bible with me to learn how to read letters such as "a, e, i, o, u", and within three months the Lord gave me the grace to know how to read that Bible fluently. But there were two places in that Bible that I didn't understand. The first one is Genesis chapter 3 where it talks about the eating of the fruit of the tree of knowledge of good and evil, and the second one is Genesis chapter 6 which tells the story about sons of God marrying daughters of men. These were very disturbing scriptures to me then and it compelled me to approach the pastor, the owner of the cows, to explain to me the meaning of the two passages of Scripture.

The pastor explained to me that the fruit of the forbidden tree in Genesis 3 is a natural fruit but it was forbidden to be eaten. He told me that Genesis 6 was about the heavenly angels who married the earthly daughters of men and begat children who were known as "giants". But I told him that in the book of Matthew Jesus said that in the resurrection there will be no marriage because people will be like angels who don't marry. He answered that with the Bible you don't have to read it and put all your heart into it, otherwise you will become mad. So, because of this, it led me into seeking God about what he said and the Lord answered me in my prayer saying, "Those Pentecostal elders don't have the answer to those scriptures you are asking. Wait, in the near future you will get the answer to those scriptures because there was a man I have used and the answer is within his books and that man, I have already taken him."

Since I had known how to read, I began preaching in the bush and many shepherds were converted to the Lord Jesus Christ. Now, when the pastor saw that I was zealous in doing the work of God, he told me to leave the grazing of the cows and to come and preach in the church.

The Lord used me in that place such that the sick and even mad people were healed. I do remember that there was an impotent man who could not marry but he was a believer. When I was on a 3-day prayer-fast, the Lord led him to come to me and for me to pray over him, and the Lord delivered him. Later he married and now he has seven children.

As I kept on ministering in the Pentecostal church, my preaching was colliding with their teachings so much so that they got angry with me. So I had to leave Gideon and his church for Soroti town. On my way I prayed in my heart saying, "Lord now I am going to Soroti, where am I going to stay?" The Lord showed me in a vision a house where I was going to stay. On arrival in Soroti, I went straight to the house that I saw in the vision. The owner was a young believer who was not married. I told him my testimony and he told me, "You also pray for me, I need the baptism of the Holy Spirit." This I did and the Lord by His Grace baptized him with the Holy Spirit.

In Soroti town, I began preaching and a church of about 50 people was established in 1973-74 and the Lord was teaching us, telling me, "Stay as you are. Don't join any denomination for I have something for you and it is coming."

In 1975, the Pentecostals in Soroti town organized a Prayer Convention and I was elected to be one of the preachers amongst the three. All of them knew that I only preached in Ateso, but I had faith in my heart that God was going to fulfil His promise that He told me in 1971. So, I went to the convention with two Bibles, the Ateso Bible and an English Bible.

On the day that I was to preach, an Interpreter was assigned to interpret for me, from the Ateso language to English. I was the only preacher who was uneducated, but the rest of the preachers knew English well.

At the pulpit, I felt the anointing of the Lord coming into my heart, and as I opened my mouth to pray, it was in English. After praying I told the people to stand up and open their Bibles to John 1:29.

All the people were speechless, even the interpreter; they all were looking at me. When I began reading the interpreter went and sat on his chair. Then I began preaching in English for about 1 hour 30 minutes and after the sermon the Lord baptized many people with the Holy Spirit.

From that moment to date, I can speak, read and write English.

## How I got the Message of the Hour

One evening, as I was seated at the public garden with the friend whom I stayed with at his home, conversing and reading our Bibles, a student of the Soroti Flying School came to join us. He came from Kenya and was also a Pentecostal Christian. He related to us several testimonies of the mighty men of God, like Billy Graham, Oral Roberts, T. L. Osborn. Then he talked about William Marrion Branham. He told us that Branham was a prophet and that God used him mightily. I asked him, "Do you have some of his books?" He replied, "Yes, I have some of them in my room." And I requested him to go and bring them to us since the place was near. He gladly agreed and went and brought us some few copies.

After we had read those books, both of us were totally convinced that this man was a prophet of God and the two questions that I had about Genesis 3 and 6 were answered in one of the books. From that I was fully convinced that this was the Elijah who was promised to come.

The whole church in Soroti believed the Message and believers were baptized by immersion in the Name of the Lord Jesus Christ according to the Scriptures.

Since 1975 I began ministering the Message while pastoring the church and other sister churches that were established in Teso. I also changed the place of residence from Soroti town to Teso College Aloet, about 5 miles away. I left the church in the town to Samuel Elonyu who is the pastor up to this day.

In 1976, at Teso College Aloet, another church was established and I gave the pastorship to Sylvano Otuya, who got married in the same year. During that time, I established several churches in Teso though my place of residence was in Teso College Aloet. I was fulfilling my calling as an Apostle sent to my people.

## My Marriage

This was unique and miraculous. I had told God that I don't want to marry because of the nature of my calling, but the Lord told me one night, "I have a wife for you somewhere and you cannot stay single." In the dream, I told God, "You will be the one to bring that wife for me and I can't pray about that marriage because You are the one who knows where she is."

In His own way God began to deal with the sister (now my wife) from a very far village called Amusus in Amuria County (now a District) and the Lord showed me to her in dreams.

In 1977, the wife of Pastor Otuya delivered a baby girl and there was a need for a helper since both husband and wife were teachers in Teso College Aloet. So he decided to go and pick his cousin sister to come and help take care of the baby. I was staying at Otuya's place at that time.

When Otuya's cousin sister came I was away in Kapelebiyong to preach for two weeks.

One evening, as I returned, I met Bro. Otuya as he was going for his evening classes, and he told me that his cousin sister had come to help with the child. As I entered the house I met the sister. Upon seeing me, before I could even greet her, she collapsed. I was amazed as to the cause. But I left her there and went to my room and began praying, thanking God for my journey mercies. Later, I went to take a shower and then went to the sitting room and found the sister had recovered. She came and greeted me.

However the revelations she had, kept torturing her for she understood that I was the man who was to be her husband whom the Lord had been revealing to her. As pressure increased within her heart, she decided to call me and her cousin brother Otuya together to hear her whole story. Then we checked her revelations. There were two brethren who got similar testimonies from the Lord about me marrying that sister. But since they knew that I was against marriage they kept it to themselves. So, in that course I told them that I had told the Lord that if He had a wife for me it would be Him to deal with her and to bring her to me. With these testimonies we cross checked and found out it was true.

Together with Otuya the Lord led us to go and meet her parents. Here God did another miracle. Having nothing to give as dowry, the father of the sister told us, "You take your wife and wed her but bring the dowry only when my son is grown up to marry. He would need that dowry for his wife."

We came back and the wedding was conducted on the 22nd July, 1977. Nine years later in 1986 the father of my wife came for the dowry owed to him and he found that the Lord had blessed us, given us cows through hard work of farming the land. I gave him 5 cows and 7 goats as my dowry for her daughter.

After establishing many churches in Teso region, the Lord told me and my family to go back to Karamoja. I shared with the brethren this testimony. As we were preparing to leave, the brethren in Teso argued with me to leave my family behind and that I was to first go and prepare a place for the family, then come back and take them. But I refused and told them that the Lord has told me to go back there with the family.

## Beginning of the Ministry in Karamoja

In December 1987, we left Teso for Karamoja and during that time there were wars. The rebels in Teso would kill people they met on the road. We had to travel in convoy and the vehicles of the army men were there to escort the convoy.

It seemed that the Devil intended to destroy us. On the way the rebels attacked our convoy and they fought with the army men but they were defeated. The tyre of our vehicle even had a puncture but all in all, God kept us safe.

Before we left Teso, God had instructed us to go and stay in Moroto District Police Barracks, saying that there was a house for us. This was in a dream to my wife. By faith we arrived in Moroto at night at around 10:00pm and when we came out of the bus, we didn't know where to go even though I had stayed in Teso for very many years. Then my family and I gathered along the road side and I told them, "Let us pray and let God lead us to where we can sleep."

After the prayers, I saw a man coming from Moroto Hospital and the voice told me to call him and ask for the whereabouts of the house of someone called Grace, who was our friend in Teso and who was posted to work in Moroto. We called the man and he pointed to us the direction to the house. He even assisted us in carrying our luggage to the house. Grace was very happy to see us. She took us into her house and we were there with her for one month.

During that time I told her that the Lord had told us to stay in the Police Barracks. I requested her to see the police officer-in-charge for a house for us. She went to enquire and was asked if the man was a Christian? With the answer given that I was one, the officer-in-charge told her that they had only one "Unipot" (a single roomed, metallic made house usually used by the police) near the "armoire" (where they keep the guns and ammunitions) and that I could stay in it.

We were taken there and stayed for two weeks but next to this house was a big house which was "bushy" and vacant. I asked the people around for the reason why the house was unoccupied. The answer given was, "It is full of demons because the officer who lived there during Amin's regime had magical charms, but when Amin was overthrown, the officer took off but those demons/spirits of his remain in the house, and seven people have lost their lives in that house."

I went to the police officer-in-charge of the barracks and told him that that vacant haunted house was the one I was supposed to live in. We had an argument for he was reluctant to let me have the house. In the end the Police Officer relented and said, "Here are the keys, if you and your family should die then your own blood is upon you."

After receiving the keys, I went and reported to my wife. We went and opened the door of the house. The house was dirty and had a foul smell.

We sensed evil presence.  Standing there we began praying and casting away those spirits. We heard the sound of footsteps running as the evil spirits left the house.  Then we washed the house and brought in our belongings.

The following morning at about 5:00am, the Police Officer came to check if we were still alive. On knocking the door he called out, "John Mark, are you alive?"  I replied, "Yes, we are alive." We opened the door and he came in.  He asked, "Under what power can you stay in this house when seven other people had lost their lives in this house?"  I replied, "Yesterday I told you that He that is in us is greater than he that is in the world and that we are occupying the house by the power of Jesus and according to the revelation which He gave us."

Then the officer said, "I am going to tell my superiors about all these happenings." Later he came back with the District Police Commander and Regional Police Commander.  With them were other people who were excited to know the things that had happened.  We testified to them of our stand in the faith.  It satisfied the officers and they gave us a license to preach the Gospel throughout the whole Region of Karamoja, and they said, "Should anyone dare stop you, report to us and we shall arrest them."

Since 1988, I began ministering the Gospel in

that house for two years to the people of Karamoja and God honoured the preaching and the Message of the Hour went forth in its power to many villages, and many local churches have been established in all parts of Karamoja.

Amongst the converts were the ring leaders of the raiders (cattle rustlers). Illiterate as they were, God gave them the ability to read and write in the local languages and are now very committed (staunch) believers and ministers of the Gospel of Jesus Christ.

Most interestingly, these ring leaders surrendered all their guns (self-disarmament) to the Government, took up the Bible and are now preaching the Gospel of Christ and disseminating the Message of the Hour with liberty in just about any part of Karamoja, Teso, Lango and Acholi regions. There are 12 established churches in Moroto District, 5 in Kotido District, 6 in Abim District, 4 in Nakapiripirit District, and many others are coming up.

To the whole population of Karamoja, amidst ethnic differences, the Gospel has brought, served and broaden unity both between the believers and non-believers, whereby if one from Bokora moves to Matheniko or Jie and he or she is a believer, one is often welcomed with joy and the unbelievers would confess to them that they are not their enemies. Hence, the Gospel of Jesus Christ has been and is the only power to transform the people of Karamoja.

Intermarriage among the different clans is not common. However, by God-given revelations, there is an increased unity through such intermarriage amongst the believers who live far apart from each other. The power of the Gospel has worked in many villages, and the believers are experiencing a transforming power with many people receiving salvation. Many non-believers confess that it is this Gospel that can liberate them and those in the villages in the far interior region where no foreign missionary ever enters, are desiring to be ministered to.

The ministering of this Gospel to the villages far and wide is done by ministers who have to walk from village to village, even to the kraals far into the interior places of Acholi, Lango, Teso and beyond the borders to Turkana land in Kenya.

# II

# TESTIMONIES OF BELIEVERS

# Called out of Denominationalism
## *By Robert Ojangole*

It was sometime in the early 1990s when the region where I lived was engaged in tribal battles. One day whilst sitting down with a police officer I suddenly had a gun shot pass through my shoe, which got blown up. I thought I had lost my foot. I was in shock and as I screamed aloud a liquid poured into my mouth, chocked me, and got swallowed through my gullet. It was the brain fluid of the policeman I was with. It gushed out of him when a bullet blew his head.

I ran home. My siblings were crying at me supposing that maybe one of the bullets had gone through my body. But by the grace of God I didn't even have one scratch on my body. It was God calling me to salvation. Desiring to now serve God I started going to the Church of Uganda.

In January of 1992 I had the following strange dream:

I was sitting in a bedroom. A filthy looking and naked woman entered the room. She was speaking enticing words to me. She kept moving around the room in her nakedness, speaking nasty things. I sat still as I looked at her. She afterwards left the room. I was still sitting down and watching what was going on when another woman entered the room. But this one was different. She was very modest;

she had a long dress and with a veil on her head. She sat on the bed. At that point a voice spoke into the room saying, *"Arise, suck from her breasts!"* Immediately I stood up and went to suck.

I woke up feeling so confused about the strange dream. I knew it had a spiritual significance. I asked the priest at my church for the interpretation but he didn't know the meaning of the dream. Then it so happened one day that the Bishop of Canterbury visited our region and I managed to find a chance to see him. I narrated the experience and asked him to help me with the interpretation of the dream. He explained words that I couldn't understand and I can't even remember them today.

Then sometime in March of 1992  a stranger visited me and requested to spend a night at my house. He was a stranded Message believer looking for the house of a brother John Mark Louse. This man then invited me to attend their church service at which Pastor John Mark was to be preaching. Reluctantly I accepted the invitation and we went together for church.

During this service brother John Mark went to the pulpit and began to preach from the book of Revelation chapter 17. What he said in this sermon forever changed the course of my life:

"A woman represents a church. A true church of God has the Word of God which dresses them with righteousness. A church without the true Word of God is a naked woman!….Elshadai God is a breast-feeding God who can feed His children with milk!"

The preaching pierced straight to my heart as it exactly answered the questions I had over my dream. That day I got baptised in the Name of the Lord Jesus Christ.

I now help Pastor John Mark to minister in the church. God bless my brother, Andrew Phiri, who communed with me in my house in Moroto, Karamoja.

## Miraculous Healing
### *By Jesse M. Nzima*

I remember one Saturday morning, during the period of Brother John Mark's visit to Lusaka, in the year 2014, I suddenly developed stomach pains. The pains didn't seem serious at the time but as the day progressed the discomfort intensified.

We were scheduled to have meetings at Brother Andrew Phiri's home later that Saturday afternoon. The home was about 10 kilometres away from where I lived. I realized that I would not be able to make it for the gathering because of the sickness and so I told my wife and the young girl we kept in the house (her niece) to proceed for the gathering.

I went to bed that night with the same problem and I was hopeful it would improve by morning.

Sunday morning came and there was no improvement. We were scheduled to have a double service that Sunday. I again advised my wife to go to church without me as my condition was not improving. The brothers at church learnt of the problem the previous day. Since I'm a very expressive and noisy person, it was apparent that my absence was felt.

When my wife left for the service that is when Satan buffeted me and the real battle with diarrhoea started. I would not last five minutes before racing back to the toilet. This went on for about six hours continuously.

This kind of diarrhoea was unusual. I later noticed that the appearance and smell of stool changed. There was now a very bad stench of non-stop black stool. I lost strength and my anal area was burning. I started feeling weak and drowsy.

I lay back on my bed and started asking God to have mercy on me. I remember praying as if I was dying as the situation proved helpless. I prayed for so many things including many people I knew and family members. I asked God to have mercy on them. I also asked Him to forgive me for the things I had not done right and for the people I had not helped in my walk with God to witness my faith.

Then between 1 and 2 PM in the afternoon, something happened to me (before this I had desired for Brother John Mark to come pray for me as he was scheduled to pray for people with different needs): I heard some faint voices and laughter approaching my gate and I knew it was brothers coming over to see me during the lunch break. My heart suddenly leaped for joy. As soon as I heard the voice of Brother John Mark, I felt a thing run away - literally running away! - from my stomach and through my anal area. The problem immediately left me and I knew I was healed. This happened just before the brothers entered the house.

After entering the house Brother John Mark offered a simple prayer. I told him that I would accompany the brothers to church after that. After I said that, Brother John Mark told me that I had done a good thing to obey God's voice by not staying in bed after the prayer. Now you know that when you have severe diarrhoea, a public place is one place you don't want to hang around. Thoughts started flooding my mind and I asked myself if I knew what I was doing but my heart was too overwhelmed with joy to entertain that kind of reasoning. I went on to attend the second service and to my surprise I didn't have the problem again. I started thinking that maybe it would start in the evening but it didn't! I remember Brother John Mark looking at me after the service and assuring me that the problem was over and that it would never trouble me again.

On the way home I was carrying my wife's bags and one of our twin boys in my hands. Brothers John Mark and Andrew Phiri looked at me from brother Phiri's car, and brother John Mark jokingly said, "Look at how this man is confidently and energetically carrying bags, who would know he had diarrhoea a while ago?" I could not hold back my laughter.

The Lord did a miracle that day. But all this was on the basis of my faith; I had confidence in the gift God had put in Brother John Mark. I believe he can do it for you.

*"But without faith it is impossible to please him: for he that cometh to God must believe that he is, and that he is a rewarder of them that diligently seek him"* (Heb. 11:6).

*"Jesus said unto him, If thou canst believe, all things are possible to him that believeth"* (Mar.9:23). Amen.

## 'Faith-full' life
### *By Andrew C. Phiri*

Brother John Mark's everyday lifestyle was characterised by faith. Faith was not a religious sentiment but his everyday reality. One day I took a long walk with him, going to trading places and moving around the various avenues of the place where I stay. On our way back home, we reached a point where two roads merged forming a "V", and I jokingly asked Brother John Mark: "If you were dropped here at night and you were all alone, show me if you can remember where our house is!" He answered, "I can't be lost. If that were to happen, the Lord will send me an angel to lead me to your house."

During this time, when Brother John Mark visited us, my wife, Norah, was expecting our second son, Terry. It was a troublesome pregnancy. She was getting dehydrated as she always vomited about every hour or so. This problem went on into the third month of the pregnancy. Before Brother John Mark came she had been admitted for medical attention. Her condition had worried and stressed me up.

One evening Brother John Mark explained saying, "Even if others would take such problems to be a normal pregnancy problem, you ought to have the faith to ask the Lord to take it away". He then testified to us of how his wife also used to vomit and would go into problems with her earlier pregnancies but when he sought the Lord and prayed for her, the problem ceased.

Brother John Mark then prayed for Sister Norah, asking the Lord to stop the vomiting problem. It was a simple prayer but an unusual thing happened:

As he prayed sister Norah felt a strange movement in her womb and she never vomited again from that moment!

# III
# TRANSCRIBED SERMONS

# EDITOR'S NOTE

*"The Lord gave the word: great was the company of those
that published it"*
(Psa.68:11)

This section of the book contains three sermons preached by the late John Mark Louse in 2014 when I had invited him to Zambia and had arranged for him to visit different places in the country. His itinerary was to also extend to neighbouring Zimbabwe.

Our hearts were glad to receive the brother. The messages of Brother John Mark were so great a blessing to our local assembly that we thought it necessary to have those which had been recorded in audio format get transcribed for people who may not understand his Ugandan accent.

The transcription is unabridged. However, any place in the text where three dots appear between words is an indication of the failure by the editor to clearly hear John Mark's accent. Words in italics or square brackets in some places indicate slight editing to make sentences understandable. You can access the audio file of this sermon on our website.

The transcribed sermons are made available to you with hope that you will be stirred to walk circumspectly in this late hour. If you are blessed through reading this work we will be glad to hear your testimony.

Your brother in Christ

Andrew  C. Phiri
December 11, 2019

## Simeon

[1] And, many of them actually are people who have never gone to school, brothers and sisters. So, what they did, they also desired to believe according to my testimony. And now those thirty churches, the ministers who are there, pastors, evangelists, all of them I can say, they know how to read and they have never gone to school. So, my testimony actually set them on fire. They believed it and asked God to give them also the grace to know how to read. So at least they are now reading. Including many of the sisters also, they know how to read the Bible.

[2] So, actually, when they heard about this journey many of them sent greetings, those who knew. So, I just want before we read the Scriptures, there is a testimony which I want to give. You know the Bible says, "when you come together, if one has a testimony, if one has a song, if one has a teaching, let everything be done for the edification of the Body".[1]

[3] So, there was a testimony which happened to us last December. Christmas was supposed to be on Wednesday, then on Tuesday I had gone to the garden. You know I have a garden of fruit trees; *it has* oranges and mangoes. So that morning of Tuesday I went to the garden; I was weeding those

---

[1] 1 Cor.14:26

trees. It came time that I was talking to myself. I said, "Lord, you are God who is so rich, you have animals in the whole bush there. I really desire that this Christmas you could give us one animal from your animals in the bush so that we can use it for Christmas.

[4] So, after talking to the Lord I came back home. Then that evening, the evening of the Tuesday, my daughter came with her husband; they came home to join us for Christmas. Then the following day was now Wednesday. Many believers gathered at my place. We had some goats [and] so we enjoyed that Christmas, sharing the Word *and* testimonies.

[5] Then late around 10 *PM my son was supposed to start 'ferrying'* some believers with his vehicle to a nearby centre. *The centre is* about seven kilometres from my place. So he escorted them with his vehicle; *it's* a Pajero *vehicle*.

[6] His wife said, "Let me accompany my husband *because* on his way *back* he may be alone". So they went together, they took those believers. Then *when* coming back, on the way they got an animal. *It* was very big of this size. *It was on* the side of the road; it stood *looking* at the light *coming from the vehicle*. Then my daughter told her husband, "This is an animal!" Then now, the brother now engaged and he just knocked the animal. *It was* a very huge *animal*. His vehicle has those iron bars in the front

there which are very strong. So, he knocked it then he went back, then he came knocked it, he knocked it three times, the fourth time now the animal died. It was very huge. So, he told his wife, "Come we *take it*". It was very heavy. So, they brought it...reaching home *they narrated the incidence.*

[7] I told them, "Ahh, this is what I have told the Lord" [congregation laughs]. So, I had now to begin calling those believers *telling them,* "Please, the Christmas is still on, come tomorrow so that we can enjoy this Christmas". So they came back, we really enjoyed that Christmas using that gift the Lord gave us.

[8] Because actually when I was talking to the Lord about that animal, I was now saying, "But you see, when Branham was asking for those squirrels, he had a gun he used for killing that animal"; I was now saying to myself, "If the Lord gives me the animal what am I going to use..." So the Lord actually brought the brother with a vehicle and he used *it* to kill the animal.

[9] So, the Lord actually is mindful of our desires. You know the Bible says, "the desire of the righteous is supplied by the Lord".[2] So, I was very, very, very happy. I thanked the Lord for that.

[10] So, there is a scripture I want us to read. It's in the book of Luke chapter 2. Brother Andrew can

---

[2] Pro.10:24, Psa.20:4-5, 37:4

read for us. Before we read let us have a word of prayer.

[11] Most gracious, eternal, excellent, heavenly Father, in the great name of the Lord Jesus Christ, our saviour and Lord, we are here to approach you in this moment, praying that Father may your grace overshadow each one of us and may you Lord forgive us of all our transgressions, which all of them *are* under the blood of your Son, the blood of atonement. As we are here Lord, as I was giving my brothers the testimony of that animal, which you provided for us, which was a desire of my heart, we enjoyed it, here we are again before you, *at* your table, desiring to eat something from your own store. We pray that Lord may the Holy Ghost be present to give us that which has pleased the Father for our survival, as we move in this ... life, sojourning to come back home...Blessed Father bless the reading of the Scripture and some of the thoughts I have in my heart to pass over as edification in this humble moment. Bless each one of us, O Father, and take over, in the name of the Lord Jesus Christ we pray. Amen.

[12] Luke 2:25-32. Let's just stand as we read. [Brother Phiri reads the verses].

*And, behold, there was a man in Jerusalem, whose name was Simeon; and the same man was just and devout, waiting for the consolation of*

*Israel: and the Holy Ghost was upon him.*

*And it was revealed unto him by the Holy Ghost, that he should not see death, before he had seen the Lord's Christ.*

*And he came by the Spirit into the temple: and when the parents brought in the child Jesus, to do for him after the custom of the law,*

*Then took he him up in his arms, and blessed God, and said, Lord, now lettest thou thy servant depart in peace, according to thy word. For mine eyes have seen thy salvation,Which thou hast prepared before the face of all people; A light to lighten the Gentiles, and the glory of thy people Israel.*

[13] So we want to share briefly on this scripture we have read. As we are waiting for the coming of the Lord there are some things we have to do. And here is this brother called Simeon, he is actually someone we could get some lessons from, *lessons from* his testimony.

[14] You know Simeon is standing for a dedicated believer. Believers who are so dedicated. Because what is known as Christianity is something between you and God, and it is something that we can call a commitment of life. One has to be so much committed into this kind of a business. That's why Jesus Christ was telling his earthly parents, when they were complaining that, "why have you done

this to us, you have made us to look for you for these three days; what is wrong with you?"[3] He told them that you see, you should know that I have to be in my Father's business.

[15] So, this man Simeon, he can give us some spiritual lessons for our Christianity as we are waiting for the coming of the Lord Jesus. So the Bible says *that* this man was dedicated, he was a holy man and he was waiting for the consolation of Israel and the Holy Ghost was upon him.

[16] Yeah, so as we wait for the Lord, we should know, which type of life are we supposed to have. Because it's not just a matter of waiting, but it's a matter of waiting with a certain kind of life which is required by the Lord. Because that was His first coming. So, Simeon was waiting for the first coming of the Lord Jesus. But the life he portrayed, the life he showed us, it is a life which was worthy for the coming of the Lord. So, Simeon was waiting but as he was waiting he had a life which was speaking the coming of the Lord. *This* made him a qualified person to see the Lord's Christ.

[17] So, here we can see that though there were many people in Israel who were waiting for the Messiah, they could actually not manage to see Him, they could not even manage to know Him. Why? Because they lacked qualifications! They

---

[3] Luk.2:48-49

lacked requirements. They lacked a life which could line up with the coming of the Lord. And Simeon was known, actually, has given us *an example of* that kind of life.

[18] So we are now waiting for the coming of the Lord but as we wait let's look at the life of this holy man called Simeon. And how do you get that kind of a life? You see, when sin came into humanity in the Garden of Eden it distorted *all* humanity's organs, everything in every human being was distorted, including the image which God had put upon a human being. Because when he was created He said, "I have to create a man in my own likeness, in my own image".[4] So, when sin came it smeared all that image. And not only that, it crooked all the human organs, it displaced everything until man was completely out of order. And because of that it was difficult now for human beings to worship God. So, that's why God now had to arrange ways of how He could live with His people.

[19] And now, how did Simeon *get* that kind of a life when all humanity was distorted, *was* destroyed, *people's lives* were out of shape? How did Simeon get it? That is one of the things we need to consider as we are waiting for the coming of the Lord. How did he get it?

---

[4] Gen.1:27

[20] You see, because God Himself is a restorer. He's a potter. Paul says He is like a porter; He is like a potter who gets the clay and then He has to mix the clay, and out of that clay He can make vessels according to His desire.[5] So, we can see that Simeon by the grace of God had met the Lord personally in his life. And we are told that this man was filled with the Holy Spirit, he had the Holy Spirit in him. So, that means that because of the Holy Spirit who was in Simeon, Simeon's life had been moulded, Simeon's life had been recreated, Simeon's life had been completely worked upon by the power of the Holy Ghost to fit actually the requirements which God wanted for those who are waiting for the coming of the Messiah. So, that's exactly something I desire to pass to all of us as the election to waken up our conscious as regarding the coming of the Lord.

[21] It is not just a matter of believing, but it is a matter of coming together with the creator, who can handle your life, lesson after lesson, stage after stage, until you become a qualified vessel to see the promises of God for your life. So, that is exactly what you need.

[22] You know, Christianity is something which everyone of us must really take with commitment; you take it with the commitment. It is something

---

[5] Rom.9:20-23

that involves all your time! And that's why Apostle Paul used to talk about redeeming the time for the days are evil.[6] But you see, the time of many people has been stolen by the enemy until there is a need to redeem. You see, because if the Devil has put your time in his pocket and he is the one handling it then you never do anything which God desires you to do with your day, and because of that, there is no time with you because the enemy has taken it, because he is a thief, he can steal it.

[23] So this man Simeon had utilised his time. His time was not stolen by the enemy. It was not stolen by the activities of the day. His time was not stolen by even his own physical body, because our physical body also is an enemy, which normally steals away our time, until we end up living a life which is ...

[24] So here we need to see very, very accurately this man Simeon, and consider very much, how did he manage to get that kind of a life? A life of that kind, how did he get it? He got it by total surrender of himself, his time, his activities to the Lord. We need to have a total surrender of ourselves to the Lord.

[25] You know, Apostle Paul when he was addressing many of the believers, you can check his writings from many of those churches, but there is

---

[6] Eph.5:16

one in Romans 12:1-2. Brother Andrew you can read [Bro. Andrew Phiri reads]:

*I beseech you therefore, brethren, by the mercies of God, that ye present your bodies a living sacrifice, holy, acceptable unto God, which is your reasonable service.*

*And be not conformed to this world: but be ye transformed by the renewing of your mind, that ye may prove what is that good, and acceptable, and perfect, will of God.*

[26] Yes, exactly! You see, the presentation of our total being to the hands of the creator is what brings out this type of a life which Simeon is portraying to us. A total presentation of our lives to the Lord. You see, because sin distorted all the humanity. And now, when the Lord gives you grace to come to Him by the power of the Gospel you need to do what Paul *says here* – "I beseech you therefore, brethren, by the mercies of God, that ye present your bodies a living, holy, acceptable sacrifice to the Lord".

[27] That's exactly how we can get that kind of a life which this man called Simeon is showing us. It's a total surrender. It's a total surrender! It's a business of its own kind. It's a business *out of* which God Himself is desiring to have a profit. Because when He comes He has to find out that you have done the business until now, the profit you can present it to

the Lord. Because the profit you are going to get, it is both *yours* and the *Lord's*. It's actually a profit to God and also a profit to yourself. Because once you surrender yourself totally to the Lord, *if* you commit yourself totally to the Lord, you are going to get a lot of profit. And the profit on your side is what we are seeing in the life of Simeon. That's the profit of living a life of sacrifice, it's a great profit!

[28] I always tell the believers, Please make sure you know what Christianity is. Because another problem is that we came into salvation and remained not understanding, not knowing, not having a revelation of what Christianity really is. Because if you see, *what happened* in the Garden of Eden brought into humanity things which are not good. Then you need a total surrender to the Lord so that those things can be done away in your life. Because what entered into us because of the Fall, all that was of Satan entered into us, all that was of the Serpent entered into us. Now, to offload all that out, you need to mean business, so that Lord Himself can have an opportunity to work His works in you until nothing of Satan, nothing of the Serpent remains hanging in you. Because they want to have a total preeminence over your being.

[29] And that is what we can see in the life of Simeon. So, he was waiting for the coming of the Lord. But as he was waiting he had something to be

admired. He had something which is a living testimony. He had something which could not bring shame to him. Because as Jesus came, that first coming, many people missed Him *a* hundred miles! They really missed Him. Even when the wise men came to Jerusalem, they said, "Please, can you show us where is the king?".[7] They said, "Which king?"They said, "We are here, we have been following the star, but where is exactly the place where the king is to be born". They told them that for us we don't know anything. Until they had to call all the hierarchy of  churches to come and explain … When they came they began opening the books, opening the books, until they discovered that it was prophesied by the prophet that you Bethlehem, though you are small, out of you will come out a ruler. Then they said, "Oh, it is supposed to be Bethlehem!" Then the wise men left. As they came to the road the star appeared. But you see, those wise men were one of the people who saw the coming of the Lord. That first coming. No wonder their message was such a mystery to many people until they could not know where has He been born from.

[30] So, as we look into the life of this man called Simeon, we can use his life as a key for us to understand, from the Scriptures, those other men

---

[7] Mat.2:1-2

and women, who actually had lived that kind of a life before, because there are many in the pages of the Word. So, we can come to people like Job, that old man. The very type of life Simeon is showing us is the very life which that man called Job had. And we could say that those were people who were qualified to become the members of the Bride of Jesus Christ. Because you cannot become a member of the Bride of Jesus Christ if you have not qualified, if this type of life is not in you. You cannot be counted as a member of the Bride of Jesus. Then it will require you and me to utilize all our time for this thing.

[31] Because Jesus used to say, there was a man, he was looking for riches, he bumped into a garden and there he got riches in that garden, he went back and sold everything in order to come and buy that garden.[8] Christianity is such a great precious thing which needs the selling of all. It requires you and me to sell all, all! You sell everything in order to redeem that kind of life which Simeon *had*. You need to sell all, because if you don't sell all, those things are going to become a road-block before you, to hinder that kind of life which God requires of us.

[32] So, we need to have Him with us, and not only that, we need to give Him all the time concerning

---

[8] Mat.13:44

our life. So that He could do away with the old thing. As Paul says, "If anyone is in Christ he's a new creature, old things have been washed away and are past but new things have come".[9] You see, in another *place in Scripture* he said, "We need to put off the old man and his works…put off that man" and then he says, "put on the new one".[10] So in order for us to attain to this type of a life, there is a 'total putting off' and a 'total putting on'.

[33] That's exactly what we can *learn* from this man called Simeon. There are great lessons there. Read for us Luke 10:38-42. [Brother Phiri reads the scripture].

*Now it came to pass, as they went, that he entered into a certain village: and a certain woman named Martha received him into her house. And she had a sister called Mary, which also sat at Jesus' feet, and heard his word.*

Now, I want us to mark that scripture. Okay, go ahead. Verse 39, that scripture there.

*And she had a sister called Mary, which also sat at Jesus' feet, and heard his word.*

*But Martha was cumbered about much serving, and came to him, and said, Lord, dost thou not care that my sister hath left me to serve alone? bid her*

---

[9] 2 Cor.5:17
[10] Eph.4:22-23

*therefore that she help me.*

*And Jesus answered and said unto her, Martha, Martha, thou art careful and troubled about many things: But one thing is needful: and Mary hath chosen that good part, which shall not be taken away from her.*

[34] Amen. Yeah. So here we could realise that in order to get that kind of life which Simeon is showing us by his personal testimony, we need to have what we can call, we should have the desire which this woman had.  You know, Mary, if you read very well her story, because when you go back to Luke Chapter 7, you will discover that this Mary here is that woman who was a great harlot in that city. She is the one who came to Jesus in the house of Simon the leper, because Simon had invited his friends and Jesus was included, to come to his house for dinner. Then as people came, he managed to wash the feet of the rest of his visitors, but when it came to Jesus' feet he ignored it. He did not wash the feet of Jesus.

[35] Then this Mary here, being a harlot, she had heard about Jesus. And Mary did, she got all the money to buy a very costly ointment in a shop. And then she brought it. So, when she came to the hall where the visitors had gathered she came straight to Jesus. She came weeping, she came crying, and she poured the oil on Jesus, all the oil, on Jesus, until

all the house was filled with that smell of the ointment. Until even His disciples got annoyed. They talked and said, "Why is this costly ointment wasted in this manner?"[11]

[36] They called it waste. But Jesus told them, "Why do you trouble the woman?" because they were actually even removing her; "Why are you spoiling this precious thing, just pouring there, you have wasted!" Jesus said, "Leave that woman alone". He gave a question to Simon, He said, "Simon, I have something to talk to you". Then Simon said, "Okay, you speak Lord". He said, "There was a man who had two *debtors*. One had taken much money, about a million *and the other only took* a *little amount.* But when these people could not pay the owner, *they came* humbly and crying saying, 'Please we have no way to pay, please can you do something'. And the man just forgave all of them". Then Jesus said, "Now Simon, of the two, which one do you think will love the master more?" Then he said, "I believe it will be the one who had *owed* much". Then Jesus said, "You see, this woman, as you see, had done great sins, so much! And that's why you can see, all what you are seeing her doing, which looks like a waste, it is just because she has done a lot of sins", and that is a bait with God ofcourse, "and some people have done sins but not

---

[11] Luk.7:37-50, Joh.12:3-5

like this woman, and all of them can be forgiven".

[37] So here now is the woman. This woman knew that there were so many things which the enemy had put in her. And now, since I have got the master I have to sit, so that I can be transformed. You can see that now. So to keep the type of life which Simeon is having, according to the testimony we are reading, we need to sit at the feet of God.

[38] And we are told this man called Simeon had the Holy Ghost and that is God Himself. And because this man Simeon has been sitting at the feet of the Holy Ghost all his lifetime, because I believe from his youth he has been just with God...until time came when the Lord told him, "You are not supposed to die before seeing the Lord's Christ". But that was the time now when the Lord had completed a mission in his life. You know each one of us must give God opportunity to do His mission of changing us into His original image which was there before, which was smeared by sin, which was distorted by sin, which was defiled by sin.

[39] So, Paul is telling us that I beseech you brethren that you must present yourself. And "to present yourself" we can see it in ... that is true presentation of *oneself* to the Lord...to get a life which qualifies him or her to become a member of the Bride of Jesus Christ.

[40] You see, because that is the highest kind of a

level. Paul calls it the "high calling", in the book of Philippians[12]. He says it's a high calling. And actually, that's God's intention *of* why the Gospel has to be preached. It is to call people to that kind of a high calling of becoming the Bride of His Son, Jesus Christ. But you cannot reach that kind of a level without sitting at the feet of Jesus Christ, as a disciple to be worked upon until you qualify for that level.

[41] So as we are waiting for His coming there is something to be done! More especially we who are living in the end time. Because the true revelation of God's Word, once the rest of the apostles passed away, it was distorted, it was wrinkled, it was destroyed until it could not be seen anymore. But God being God, He had talked through His prophets concerning the restoration. And in this end-time He gave us a messenger who was a prophet-messenger... A man with a prophetic office, in which Jesus Christ actually came into, in order to fulfil a sign which happened to Abraham before the destruction of Sodom and Gomorrah.

[42] You see, so God came to us through this messenger and He has brought a restoration of the original. And since we are now going back to the book of Acts, so what do we need? A true total commitment in order for God to achieve that kind

---

[12] Phi. 3:14

of life He desires *for His sons*.

⁴³ So this man Simeon he has lessons which we can pull one by one to ourselves, one by one, one by one, until we come exactly to the standard of that life. Because that is the standard of the Bride. It is the standard of the Bride to reach that kind of a life. And you cannot reach it with a lazy type of life. You know ... people *live* a lousy lazy type of life. And, if it requires, in the physical, for you to labour and sweat as a farmer until you get the food, what of the spiritual things? You must be dedicated, you must labour! You must commit yourself until you begin to … from God what is required for yourself, and that is what Simeon actually did here.

⁴⁴ I like very much the testimony of this man called Simeon because it's a key kind of a life. Once you see what Simeon is portraying, is revealing, is showing, you can go deep into other scriptures, into other vessels of God which lived before him, you could see that truly these are people called the Bride. Because that is the only way you can actually enter to the … of the Bride.

⁴⁵ You know, and most especially the believers of this Message, they need to be taught; *there are those with an attitude of religion.* They say, "Since we have believed the prophet that's all". Brothers it's not all! You have to take this Christianity as a

duty. As a duty! You know in the book of Ecclesiastes[13] Solomon says, "Let us hear the conclusion of the matter, and this is it; Fear God, keep His commandments, and this is a duty for all men". It's a duty!

46 It's a duty that you commit yourself to these things until you see the power of God working in your life day and night, day and night, day and night. Now, as He is working you are going to see yourself climbing a ladder to reach a standard.

47 There is a standard set by God for all His children. And all those who fail to reach *it* will not come in the First Resurrection. They will not come! You see, because that First Resurrection has three phases and the first phase of that Resurrection has already taken off, *it was* already fulfilled when Jesus rose, and the second one will come when *the* Bride of Jesus Christ will be raptured. Now, you are not going into that resurrection if you *lack such a life.* It is something we have to take very, very seriously!

48 And that is why I was telling Brother Andrew that, you see, as we are coming back to the book of Acts it means that we are coming back to the church of Ephesus, and from the church of Ephesus we can learn that those believers were totally committed. They had what we call evening

---

13 Ecc. 12:13

fellowships, every day! From house to house, house to house, house to house, *and* on Sunday they go back to the church house. But from all those other days, every evening was utilised for the breaking of the Word. And that is exactly how the believer can reach this type of life, by eating at the table of the Word.

[49] Because even feet-washing, I mean the Communion, it is required for the believers to be taking it often, because Paul says, "as often as you do that you will be given grace to talk of the resurrection of Jesus Christ by His power until He comes, until Jesus Christ comes"[14]. You see, so, we need to see lessons which this man underwent in order to get this type of a life. He underwent a lot. A lot of dedication.

[50] Because, Christianity, one good thing I like with Christianity, it is something which actually you can enjoy even when your partner, or one who's your wife or your husband, does not know that you are enjoying, sometimes, you see, and yet you are just in the same room. Because you can just be rejoicing, praying in the Spirit, talking to the Lord; nobody can even hear your words, but you are just maybe two on the bed, you and your wife, but she or he cannot hear! It's a ...so mysterious until it takes each one of us to be committed to it.

---

[14] 1 Cor.11:26

And you cannot say, "Because my wife or my husband is committed so therefore we share the *life*". Ah no, it can't happen.

⁵¹ So Simeon, according to the Word of God, shows us from many other scriptures what we need to undergo in order to come up with that life. And actually when now you take Christianity like that then you'll surely *enjoy it*. Christianity becomes so personal! It becomes so personal until you can just enjoy it whether you are riding, whether *you are doing your gardening*, planting the cassava, or in the shop or in the office, in every work you are doing you will just be enjoying your Christianity. Because it's a commitment. It's a mystery which is so enjoyable by those who have it until they are one. Because you receive it from one source. This brother got it from the same source, *this one, that one* ... and when we gather like this, automatically He is filling us with Himself. Because our commitment leads us to that Spirit, which is one source.

⁵² So Simeon is showing us what kind of a life God is requiring *of us as* believers. Because this age we are in now, it is the age of the Rapture. And by the way, there is a lot of ignorance in this Message. People are so peaceful and yet the life they live according to the Scripture, which is the weighing machine for every activity, is totally

empty! Because, before actually I left for this journey, I got a dream which shocked me. I saw many believers – even including the ministers – they were naked. Naked totally! And then I was now wondering, "What could this be?! What is the problem? What is the meaning of all this?!" The Lord told me that "Anybody who is not baptised by the Holy Ghost is totally naked as you see!"And He referred me to Luke, I think we read that Scripture there, 24:49. He referred me to Luke, that Scripture there. Everything has shocked me, and as I am closing this testimony, I just want us to know that we need, each one of us, to be baptised by the Holy Ghost, because actually that is one of the requirements which Simeon actually had. Luke 24:49.

*And, behold, I send the promise of my Father upon you: but tarry ye in the city of Jerusalem, until ye be endued with power from on high.*

You see…until you are clothed, you are covered with the power from on high. When sin came in the Garden of Eden, it took away that garment, it took away that Holy Spirit, it took away God from Adam and Eve. And what was there, they were found naked. And that's why they begin now trying to get some kind of bras and make aprons for themselves, to cover their nakedness. So now, every believer who has come to this Truth, if he or she is not baptized by the Holy Ghost is just as naked as Adam and Eve were. Because we need to be baptized by the Holy Ghost to become our clothing.

[53] And actually when I saw that in my dream I said, "Truly we have preached for many years but we have never emphasized this point". And that's the point *which must be* emphasized, because it *enables us* to be disciples of the Lord. Because once you are baptized with the Holy Ghost then you can be a disciple of the Lord, that means you can now sit and be transformed. Because He is not going to change somebody who is not yet baptized by the Holy Ghost.

[54] And that is one of the requirements which Simeon had, he was a baptized man with the Holy Ghost, even in such a rare time when the Holy Ghost was not even poured *on* many people, but Simeon was baptized with the Holy Ghost. And because he was baptized with the Holy Ghost, "The Holy Ghost told him…the Holy Ghost *sent* him…The Holy Ghost worked on him", and brought him out as a qualified person to be *a* Bride-member.

[55] So, that is what we need in this ample time as we are waiting for the coming of the Lord. We need *to* have this kind of life. You see, because without this kind of life we are in trouble. Because the life

of Simeon is a life of total holiness and the fear of God.

[56] So, every one of us, brothers and sisters, should take this as a lesson … it's a lesson of its own, because it is actually there where the Lord can have an opportunity to work in our Christian life. First, be baptized by the Holy Ghost! Because that is actually what Simeon is showing us. He was baptized with the Holy Ghost. And when somebody is baptized by the Holy Ghost then he can be a disciple, he actually *can now* be qualified to be taught by the Lord. But if you are not baptized with the Holy Ghost there is no way the Lord can even teach you. Paul said, "A carnal man, a natural man, takes the things of the Spirit to be foolishness"[15]. You see, the things of the Spirit, the teachings of the Spirit are foolishness to that one who is not baptized by the Holy Ghost, because you are still carnal, you are still… you cannot even know the language of that hope…you cannot even know who you are. You cannot even have the … which God has ordained for you, you cannot. So, the life of Simeon has something for us in this generation, as we are waiting for the coming of the Lord.

[57] So, that is actually something very little I could leave with you, as a testimony. So let each one of us begin to pull up the socks, tighten our belts, put

---

[15] 1 Cor. 2:14

on our jackets and begin to take a serious step into this matter called Christianity! We have to take a serious step! We *should* begin so seriously as though we have just believed! And that is actually how I handle Christianity. I make it a personal recent thing. I don't even count all those years. Because I know once you begin to take Christianity like that, it has become what you can call routines *or* creeds; it has become formality, and it is no longer spiritual, because the things of God are ever with higher dimensions...Tomorrow as we come it has to be higher than *today*, higher than that, until the Rapture comes. We should know that Christianity has its own dimensions, and its own dimensions are actually arrived by the kind of attitude we have as we always stay with Him.

[58] So, as we always stay with the Lord, the kind of attitude we have should be getting like those of Mary, a life of dedication. A life of dedication is needed now in order for us to put off the worldly life, put off the worldly ways, the worldly behavior. Because *when* the Holy Ghost was calling Abraham He told him, "Separate yourself from your country, from your family, from your household, and come and I will take you to another land"[16]. We need to separate ourselves and come and meet the Lord to take us to another land, that is, a spiritual kind of a

---

[16] Gen.12:1

dimension. He wants us to reach that. That's the land He wants us to reach, which those Israelites where told to go but they could not enter because of unbelief, but few entered. So that land there types the spiritual Christianity. That's what it types. It is there where we came to be qualified as the members of the Bride, because we shall now get from the Holy Spirit all the requirements needed for us, we get from Him. As this five-fold ministry stands, when apostles stands, we get from the Spirit of God who is using the Word we get from that office, when a prophet stands we get from that office. Like that, like that, like that, until the perfection of the saints. You see.

[59] So, as I close, it is my sincere prayer that let's see this man's life, and let that life of Simeon empower us to go to the Lord in another different dimension we have never done. It requires us to take that kind of a stand. Now as I close, it'll just take me back to the time of Abraham. The Bible says, Abraham at his home in the cool of the day, he lifted up his eyes and he saw a man, three men coming from far, and he stood up and took off. When he reached there he discovered that one was God, two were angels. Then what did Abraham…

# The Way of Escape

[1] The Lord bless you church. I greet you all in the Name of Jesus Christ. I thank the Lord because am back home again, after many years. Maybe many of you were just babies, and some were not even born maybe. But I thank the Lord that He is still keeping us. I want also to thank the Lord for Brother Mawino who has been so willing to come over with me and to give me company in prayer and in all things. I want to bring greetings to you from Uganda, especially *from* my home church in Moroto. Also greetings from my family; my wife and children. And also *from* the church in Kampala, and believers in Zimbabwe and *from* Lusaka. I want to thank the Lord for all that. They sent greetings to you.

[2] We just want to read some scriptures here to share, in the book of Matthew. I am called John Mark. My name is John Mark. And then the other name is Louse. That is another name. Matthew Chapter 4. I want us here to share something that the Lord has put in my heart. Let's first have a word of prayer.

[3] Heavenly Father, in the Name of Jesus Christ, we want to give you praise and glory even this afternoon Lord. We are happy Lord because you have sustained us, you have kept us, and you have protected us Lord. Even you brought us from

Choma along the road and we are here O master! We have found our brothers and sisters gathering before you. Here we are, we present our lives unto you as a living sacrifice. We pray that Lord where we have wronged you, where we have gone astray, you forgive us all our trespasses, O Father. Bless us by the blood of the Lamb and give us the Word of Life for this evening, Lord. Minister to our souls O Father and lift us up to serve you in Spirit and in Truth. Give us the words of Life O Father…to us before thy throne of mercy. That we may hear from you. Father we shut any spirit of the enemy away from here. We call on the Holy Ghost to take the pre-eminence. And cover each one of us O father. Give us the imprest of your own Spirit and minister to us your Word. In the Name of Jesus Christ we pray. Amen.

[4] Yeah, Chapter 4 of Matthew. We shall read verse 8 and verse 9:

*Again, the Devil taketh him up into an exceeding high mountain, and showeth him all the kingdoms of the world, and the glory of them; And saith unto him, All these things will I give thee, if thou wilt fall down and worship me.*

[5] Let's also read one scripture in the first letter of John chapter 5, we shall read just one verse from there. 1 John 5:19. Let's read from verse 18 also, but verse 19 is what I desire.

*We know that whosoever is born of God sinneth not; but he that is begotten of God keepeth himself, and that wicked one toucheth him not. And we know that we are of God, and the whole world lieth in wickedness.*

[6] May the Lord bless the reading of His Word. You can be seated. Yeah, we just want to share since our time is running fast, *the only way of escape.* The only way of escape. We know that this world here is in the hands of Satan. Everything you see in the world is possessed by the Devil! And all the departments of the world, kingdoms, presidents, and whatever is there is, all *are* under the umbrella of this wicked angel called Satan. Because he told Jesus, "all the kingdoms of the world and their glory I can give you if you worship me".[17] Now, it was given to him by Adam because Adam fell off from his rulership. So, because of that everything is under the authority and power of the Devil. That makes us now to be very very careful how we walk in this world, and everything we possess and we use, we *should* know how to use it, because all of them belong to the hands of the Devil. So we are only using them because we are handling the Word of God, and by faith we use them. So because Satan is the king of this world, then there is a way of escape *from* his own pollution and all his

---

[17] Mat.4:8-10, Luk.4:5-8.

sinfulness. Because he is the one possessing everything; everywhere you go whether in college, whether in primary, whether in … Satan is powerful to influence all of them. Everything, even the dressing, even the talk, even the behaviour, everything which people do, it is by the power of Satan!

[7] So we need now to know, *How am I going to escape all these powers?* Because all these things now, we should know how to escape so that we cannot be polluted by Satan. We should have revelation! Because we as God's children we should abide somewhere in the Word of God there. That's why Jesus says, "Abide in me and my words abide in you"[18]. Because if you are not abiding in Jesus Christ and His Word, you are going to be polluted by the Devil. Because everything is just under the business of Satan. He is handling all the churches and he is twisting them for his own business and for his own sake. That is why when you enter into various churches what is done there you cannot believe. From their pastor to the deacon to the bench sitters, everything done there is so filthy! Why do people who serve God, who worship God reject the Word of God? You give them *baptism in the Name of Jesus*, they cannot understand, they cannot believe, they cannot

---

[18] Joh.15:4

receive, Why?! You give them the way apostles used to baptise[19], you give them the way the prophet use to lead, they cannot… neither can they believe. Because they are all covered by the god of this world.

[8] They are all blindfolded by the god of this world. The god of this world has given them a substitute of the Word of God. He has given them religion instead of salvation. He has given them a college instead of revelation. He has given them falsehood instead of the truth. But we should know, *How am I going to escape?* Because even if we enter into a church you are going to be polluted.

[9] There must be a church in which you can hide yourself. Which type of a church is that? The only church *which* has a revelation of God's Word, that's where you have to be! And even though you are there, you yourself must get a revelation *about* how to escape. Because this devil here is not far even from us. In the days of Job when the children of God were there to present themselves to God, Satan also came there to present himself to God. And God said, "Satan, what is your job here? What are you doing here?" [20] So you can see that there is only one way of escape, and that is what we are desiring to know now – the way of escape!

---

[19] Act.2:38, 4:12,8:16, 10:48.
[20] Job 1:6

[10] Now the only way of escape is to abide in the Word of the Lord, but not just in a *letter*, not in a parable, but in the revelation of the plan of God for you and me. Paul said, "When I came to you I didn't use excellency words of man, I don't do that. But am only coming to present to you the counsel of God".[21] The counsel of God is the revelation of God for you and it is there in the Word of God. It is by revelation how you can escape all the powers of Satan, the falsehood of Satan, and all the things of Satan. It is by revelation.

[11] Abel escaped all the falsehood of Satan in his time. How did Abel escape? Because he could not be polluted by Satan. Satan could not dirten him. Abel was a pure seed of God, worshipping God in holiness. He could not be touched. That is how he escaped, by a revelation of the Word of God. He saw Jesus Christ in the mind of God and then he brought his lamb as a substitute of Jesus Christ whom he saw. Then when God saw the sacrifice of Abel, it was a sacrifice which was having the blood, it was a sacrifice which was crying the language of the cross. It was a sacrifice which was crying the language of redemption. He was the only centre of salvation for man. There was healing in the sacrifice of Abel. There was deliverance in the sacrifice of Abel. The forgiveness of sin was hidden

---

[21] 1 Cor.2:1-5.

in that sacrifice. And when Abel slaughtered his sacrifice, and the blood came out of the throat, his sins were completely covered. Though it was not remitted, but it was covered, because his lamb was a substitute of Jesus. It was only a picture of Jesus Christ but it saved the life of Abel. It made Abel to escape all the falsehood of Satan.

[12] Yeah, he showed Jesus the glory of the kingdoms. That's why even in schools sin is done there. We take our children to school but it is sad to find out that they came back with pregnancy! What happened? We took them to school to study, to have wisdom, here they came with babies which have no fathers. And if they escape to be pregnant in the school, we take them to college *and* after finishing they go now to look for jobs. Now reaching there in the offices with their papers, that "I have a degree, I have also a diploma, I have a certificate, I am supposed to go in veterinary…" In the office there they've got a big huge devil called a boss telling your daughter, "If you want to get the job, you be my friend. These *application* letters here without you accepting what I am *telling* you are just nothing." Now the poor girl because she wants a job she accepts to be influenced by this demon, and yet this man is a house of HIV. The girl has got the job, after two to three years she is already affected, she is already dying now. This one

is completely covered by Satan.

[13] That's why he was telling Jesus, "All the glory of these kingdoms are in my hands."[22] So all our children, our sons and daughters, they must be in the Word of God if they want to escape! But the problem is that our children are not dedicated to hear the Word of God in the church. And since they are not dedicated they cannot have revelation which can help them in the time of trial, there in the offices. They have not been listening to what was spoken by the pastors. And yet what was given here it was supposed to be a revelation to guide you in your school, even in your getting your job.

[14] So we need to see where is the way of escape. It is only the Word of God. This Word of God is the one which can hide your life. Because there is no arrow which can penetrate the Word of God. Everything we see will pass away, *but* the Word of God abideth forever.

[15] How did Daniel escape the pollution in the land of Babylon (in the book of Daniel chapter one verse eight)? How did he escape? Yes, that's why it is good to be in fellowship like this, so that we are instructed *on* how to escape the pollution of the world. Because you are a different person. You are a son, you are a daughter of a king, and you are supposed to keep yourself clean! You are supposed

---

[22] Mat.4:8-9.

to live a holy life here on earth. You are supposed to look like your Father here on earth so that when time comes for you to go to him you'll have no condemnation, because you have been hiding in the Word and your life is clean. Daniel 1:8:

*But Daniel purposed in his heart that he would not defile himself with the portion of the king's meat, nor with the wine which he drank: therefore he requested of the prince of the eunuchs that he might not defile himself.*

Now, the Bible said Daniel decided that, I cannot defile myself. That is how you can escape. You have to communicate to your heart that I cannot defile myself by anything of this world here! Because all the things of the world here, they are so defiling.

[17] Anything you touch in this world here, if you don't touch it by revelation you are going to be defiled. That's why the Bible says *that* even our dressing must be by the revelation of the Word of God. Because Satan is hanging in every clothe in the shop. He has put his own shoes there in the shop, in the market. And you who is a believer, when you go to buy a shoe or a cloth, you must be led by the Spirit of God! How…how are you going to be okay in the church here when you are buying shoes which are like this?…um?…What is that?…um… What kind of shoes is that? …um?…

It is just a trap! Anytime, even when walking alone it will just break your leg. Because it is the Devil putting a trap there and yet it is a costly shoe, you buy with a lot of money, but it is a trap. And this time the clothes which are there are so transparent like nets of mosquito. If you have to buy *one for* a sister you have to buy again the inner one which is very thick, which is very heavy… now the outward is so transparent and then the inner one you have to buy another heavy one. Costly! Everything costly. So we need to know, *how am I going to escape all this pollution*?

[18] You know angels told Lot, "*You run and escape!...*" But all what was in that city looked so good. Now, all that was in the city, plus the people of the city, were wicked before the Lord. So you need to hide yourself in the Word of God. Because it is in the Word of God where our safety is. When you are in the Word of God Satan's powers are powerless to touch you! The Bible says, the Word of God is so powerful and is alive! Powerful so that anyone who has the Word of God in the heart he cannot be touched. It is so powerful that when you have the Word of God you are feared by demons.

[19] There is no church which Satan can fear. Even the Message churches today, Satan has entered and given pastors wives and wives *plus* wives! And *they* think they are rich with wives. Why? They

have not found a way of escape. And yet, the revelation of the Word of God for this day is the only escape you have to hide yourself in! You have to hide yourself in the revelation of God's Word.

[20]…The *Messenger of the Hour*, how many people approached him? They wanted to give him millions and millions of money. He refused. It is not that money is bad, but if it is money given by Satan you just reject it. I remember when I first began preaching in Karamoja. The bishop of Protestants came with his reverend *and* they called me in the office. They said, "Now John Mark it is good that you have come here…We want you to come…I want you to be here so that that church there", he was showing me a very big cathedral, "that church there, you are going to be a pastor of that church. And the diocese, the church, is going to educate your children. And every week we are going to give you food, and powdered milk, even oil, every week we are going to give your family! Come so that we preach together." I told them, I told him, "Mister bishop, thank you for all what you are talking, but do you know the one who has sent me here? I am sent here by God and God has told me, Don't enter in any denomination, Stay outside all of them!" They said, "But now how are you going to survive? Your family, you don't even work, you don't have food, how are you going to

survive? I told them, "That is not my concern. The one who sent me it is upon Him. If He sent us here to die by starvation, we are going to heaven, but going to any church I cannot." They told me, "…get out of the office. Get out of the office." I said that's okay. So, it is the Word of God which you can enter and hide yourself *in* because in the Word of God there is protection. Any person who is in the Word of God is highly protected and fenced.

[21] We are told this man called Job, when Satan was trying to ask *for* permission from God about Job's life, God told him, "Now, you don't know that Job is a very righteous man? Don't you know that he is a holy man?" Satan told God, "Does Job fear God for nothing? Haven't you put a fence around his house, around his property, around his children? And you have made all his cows, sheep, camels, and donkeys to multiply!"[23] Satan was able to see the fence which was around Job.

[22] Now, that is the only way of escape. You have to hide yourself in the revelation of the Word of God for your day! Because in the day you are in, God has moved out from every church, every denomination, and He is now in the Word of the Hour! And it is there where God is, and anybody who is in that Word of God for the Hour the fence of God is there. When Jesus met Paul on Damascus

---

[23] Job 1:8-9.

road, he knocked Paul down. And when Saul was still lying on his back, maybe on his back or in front (because he was knocked down), so when he came back from his suffocation he said, "Who are you Lord?" Jesus said, "I am Jesus whom you are persecuting. It is impossible for you to kick against the fence."[24] You cannot kick the fence. You see, the fence is in the Word of God. As long as you are in the Word of God for a day, you are fenced up! You are fenced! Diseases are out! Sin is out! Religion is out! Fear is out! Calamity is out! Sin is out! All demons are out. So you are there rejoicing, jumping, worshipping and serving the Lord, inside there. Because the fence of God is your protection against everything, even against death! Death has no power over you.

[23] That's why they threw Daniel in the den of lions. They thought that lions could just consume Daniel like bread. But when the lions reached there, when Daniel landed in the midst of the lions they could not tear his body, they could not eat his body, because he was highly protected by the power of God. Daniel was not fearing. He told the king, "The God I serve continuously He will send his angels to keep me and to shut the lion's mouth, they will never hurt me." Daniel was not worried. He was telling the king, "King, live forever, as for me you

---

[24] Act.9:4-5.

throw me there in the den, the God I serve He is more than powerful to send his angel to keep me."[25] The only way of escape! It is in the Word of God, in the revelation of the Word of God!

[24] Paul calls it "the counsel of God", that protection there, he calls it, "the counsel of God"; "I am here to deliver to you the counsel of God",[26] for your protection, for your safety. He was telling the church, "You listen to this counsel of God so that you are okay as you are living on the earth here". You see, today you find believers they are so panicking because of the world and the …which are in the world. They listen to radios and the radio says, "Oh, Ebola has come! Oh it is now here, it is coming from South Africa, is now coming from Congo, is coming from…" And the believers themselves are just panicking, "Brothers have you heard that Ebola is coming? I don't know where we can be?" You are blind against your protection! You who is in Christ, you have already escaped! You have escaped all the pollution, and the lust and the death of the world!

[25] Let's just see 2 Peter 1:3-4. It says:

*According as his divine power hath given unto us all things that pertain unto life and godliness, through the knowledge of him that hath called us to*

---

25 Dan.6:19-23.
26 Act 20:27.

*glory and virtue:*

*Whereby are given unto us exceeding great and precious promises: that by these ye might be partakers of the divine nature, having escaped the corruption that is in the world through lust.*

[26] Now Peter was declaring the only way of escape for the believer. Peter was telling them that the power of God has already given us a way out, *of* how we can escape. He said that God has given us His great promises. Because, there is power in the promises of God for the day. And your duty, my duty is to hide ourselves in the promises of God for the day. That's why every believer must be dedicated prayerfully to ask God to give you a revelation of the day, of the message of your day, now!

[27] You know the Bible says, we are students, we are disciples, we are learners, we are in the school! What are we learning? We are learning how to escape! We are learning the promises of God in which we can escape the corruption and death and sin of Satan. But the problem is that many believers are not dedicated to learn! People are so slow to go into the School of Life. Even Paul says, "We should never neglect our assembling together like others."[27] Which means even in the days of Paul there are those who neglected this escape.

---

[27] Heb.10:25.

[28] The spirit of the Devil is not asleep. In every age he has got tactics *of* how he can blindfold and weaken the church. He gives people a lazy mind, a lazy concern. That's why Paul was telling the church of Corinth, "Every time I come here I give you milk-gospel because you are babies, you cannot understand." He told them, "Up to now you are unable to understand!"[28] Why? Because the Devil, the god of this world, had cheated the church of Corinth. Because he made them babies every time. But let's know that we are in the School of Life to learn how we can escape. Because the Word of God here has everything for us.

[29] In the book of Colossians Paul says, "We are in Christ and we are hidden there".[29] We are hidden there. So you have to abide in your place of hide. It is there where your Sabbath is. Never to come out! Because outside the fence of God there are demons, there are sicknesses, there are troubles, and death is there. Anytime you step outside he will hold your leg and pull you there. Why do we see people today backsliding in the church? Boys and girls, even big men, even pastors, even ministers, why? why? They have not entered into where they can escape.

[30] You know the revelation of God's Word is like a house where you can enter and you are safe.

---

[28] 1 Cor.3:1-2.
[29] Col.3:3.

When you enter into the revelation of the Word of God the Devil is powerless to pull you out from there. He cannot enter there! That's why Peter says, "He is roaring like a roaring lion, he's running around *and* around; he wants whom he can devour".[30] Because he cannot enter. He cannot enter because you are hidden in God by a revelation. That's why Abel could not be defiled; he could not be polluted because he was inside the revelation of God. And that's why Satan was unable to catch him. The only way of escape!

[31] Because when you enter in the revelation of God you can stay peaceful and restful. You know Jesus said, "Come to me and I will give you rest".[31] There is rest in that revelation! Once you have the revelation you can rest, all demons can roar like lions but they cannot tamper with you. Yes, people can backslide, they can go for denominations because of money, but that spirit will not tamper with you because you yourself you are hiding yourself in the revelation of God's Word where Satan has no power to pull you out. He cannot touch you. The only way of escape!

[32] Shadrack, Meshack and Abednego knew the way of escape. Satan had brought a picture to be worshipped, an image, the very image of Daniel.

---

[30] 1 Pet.5:8.
[31] Mat.11:28.

He told them, "You worship this man, he's my God, because he gives me interpretation of dreams".[32] But those boys were in the revelation of God and because of that they had escaped that. Now, today sin is covering the whole face of the earth. There is falsehood, hypocrisy is covering everywhere. But it's only those who have the revelation of the Word of God, they are the only one who can escape that. That's why today we see the whole world has HIV. People are dying every day. But David said, "Even if death can come on all sides *it* cannot touch me".[33] The only way of escape.

[33] Now, we have talked about the Word. Let's see Acts 1:8:

*But ye shall receive power, after that the Holy Ghost is come upon you: and ye shall be witnesses unto me both in Jerusalem, and in all Judaea, and in Samaria, and unto the uttermost part of the earth.*

Now, the way of escape is to be in the Word of God and in the Spirit of God. Yeah, Jesus said, "When the Holy Spirit comes upon you, you will have power". We have talked about the Word, let's talk little again about the Holy Spirit. This Spirit here, Jesus said it's the Spirit of Power. When you

---

[32] Cf. Dan.2:47-48, 3:1-6.
[33] Psa.91:7

are inside this Spirit you are protected by the power of God. That Spirit there, it is a spirit of power. There are no other powers which can overcome this other power here. That's why John the revelator, the Bible says he was beaten *but* could not die. He could not die. Until they decided to cook him with grease, *for* twenty-four hours. Now when John could not die, they got him out of the drum and took him to Patmos. They said, "This man is a wizard, Let *us* put *him* there, to die there!" Because they could not kill the Holy Spirit, which is power, which was in John. God had purposed life so that He could give him  to write the whole of the book of Revelation.

[34] Because Paul had talked that there are things which the eye has not seen, no ear has heard, it has not entered in man's heart.[34] They are there given by God and kept by God, it will be revealed by the Holy Ghost. So, John was to go to Patmos. So when he went there Jesus now came and said, "Now you write my book, write the revelation".[35] And he was there for two years writing the book of Revelation. He *wrote* that book with pictures and all this type you are seeing here. But it was a letter of God to the Bride! So, John was full of the Holy Spirit. And because he was full of the Holy Spirit he escaped

---

[34] 1 Cor.2:9.
[35] Rev.1:10-11.

all, even death! He could not be polluted.

[35] So when you have the Holy Spirit you have escaped! Because the Holy Spirit is your protection. He is there to protect you against sin, against pollution, against death. And those who are in the Holy Spirit they cannot fear anything. So, that is where we have to enter in. That's the way of escape. And by entering there you have actually defeated Satan. See, in Revelation *chapter* Six here, I want us to read one scripture there. Revelation 6:6. Let's begin with verse 5 but its verse 6 that I want:

*And when he had opened the third seal, I heard the third beast say, Come and see. And I beheld, and lo a black horse; and he that sat on him had a pair of balances in his hand.*

*And I heard a voice in the midst of the four beasts say, A measure of wheat for a penny, and three measures of barley for a penny; and see thou hurt not the oil and the wine.*

[36] Now, I want us to see, the voice says, Don't hurt the oil, don't hurt the wine! The way of escape. You know, the oil represents the Holy Spirit. And wine represents the stimulation, the anointing of the Holy Spirit. Now, it is there where we have to be in to escape. Be in that oil, the Holy Spirit. Be in that wine, the anointing of revelation. So, when you are there, when I am there, there is no arrow which can

enter there. No blade which can enter there. Because the Lord who is oil and wine will be our fence. And all who are in the oil, in the wine, are kept by angels of God. God has given charge to angels to keep them. We are told by King David in Psalm 34:7 that the angel of the Lord encamps around those who fear God and He will deliver them!

[37] So as long as you are in the oil and the wine the angels of God are there to keep you. Just like He kept Daniel. Just like He kept Shadrack, Meshack, and Abednego. They were in the wine, in the oil. It is only the oil and the wine which cannot be touched by Satan. So when you are inside there you are untouched. If you are outside there, Satan can kick you like a ball, from East, West, and South. Because you have no escape. You have no protection.

[38] Another way of escape is to have the name of Jesus Christ with you. Jesus has given us His name. You know the name "Jesus" is the name "Joshua", it's actually the name of God, the name of redemption, the name of protection, the name of power! That's why Jesus says, "I come in my Father's name!"[36] That was the name of God. That's why God has given us His name, and that name is Jesus! When we have that name gates of

---

[36] Joh.5:43.

hell will never *prevail against* us. That's why Jesus said, "Go and cast out devils in my Name!"[37]

[39] Yeah, *there is* no demon who does not understand the name of Jesus. In the days of Paul there was a certain priest called Sceva. And he *had* seven boys. But those boys were not saved. The priest was not saved also. So, they went to a mad man. A mad man who was naked and the seven boys surrounded the man. They said, "Satan, we cast you in the name of Jesus whom Paul is preaching!" Those demons listened. "Satan, we cast you in the Name of Jesus whom Paul is preaching!" Then the Devil said, "I know Jesus. I know Paul. But who are you?" Before they could answer he had removed their clothes away.[38] That devil removed all their clothes away, and shoes, and he had beaten them, the blood was falling, until everyone *had to get to the door to run out*. Because it was inside a house. The Bible says they went out naked and bleeding. Yeah, demons know Jesus. That's the name which God has given us on earth here for our redemption, for our healing, for our protection, for our defeat of demons. It's the name you have to breathe in the battle! You know David said, "I come to you Goliath in the Name of the

------

[37] Mar.16:17.
[38] Act 19:11-17.

Lord!"[39] That is the name of the Lord. The name of the Lord of hosts. And that's why Jesus Christ was the warrior. He came to conquer all demons, He conquered death, He conquered the grave, He conquered hell. He came with the keys! So He gave us His name. Now, because we are the Bride of Jesus, we have been actually married to Christ and we have now His name.

[40] Another thing which is our escape, let's read one scripture as we close, the book of Revelation. Let's see something in the book of Revelation. Revelation 12:11. That will be my last scripture now. Revelation 12:11:

*And they overcame him by the blood of the Lamb, and by the word of their testimony; and they loved not their lives unto the death.*

Now, here, another thing I want us to put there is the blood of the Lamb. The blood of the Lamb is another thing, you have to have it for escape. Because that was the blood which was poured for our redemption. Now, if the blood of bulls and goats could cover the sins of the Israelites what about the blood of Jesus Christ, the blood of the Lamb now? It's the blood which can remit our sin. The blood of animals used to cover but the blood of the Lamb remiteth! It completely expels until you

---

[39] 1 Sam.17:45.

don't look as a sinner; you look holy.

[41] So, when you come and take the name of Jesus Christ as your name of redemption the blood of Jesus takes away your sin; before God you are holy, you can fellowship with God. Then the blood of Jesus Christ is there to be your own covering. Paul says, "We have boldness to enter the Holy of Holies by the blood of Jesus, without fear!"[40] That's why every time when you kneel, when you pray, even in the car, even around the garden, even in your office, when you pray, the blood of Jesus is there to cover you! To make you acceptable before God in your prayers! Yeah, even when you are attacked by spirits, just say, "Oh, the blood of Jesus! The blood of Jesus! The blood of Jesus!" You are going to see those demons taking off.

[42] Just the blood of Jesus only, every devil will get his way to run, because that is the blood of God. Because in the womb of Mary God made a body for Himself and put His own blood there, in that body! That's why Jesus, He could die and resurrect because He was innocent from sin. He had no sin, in fact no *Original Sin* in Him. He was the only holy who was declared to be the Son of God, by the Spirit of holiness. He was the only accepted by the Father to do the work of redemption for God's children who were taken *into* captivity by the Devil.

---

[40] Heb.10:19-20.

The only way of escape. Be there!

[43] Though there are many other things we could touch but I just want us to remain there, to know how we can escape. If you are in this salvation, if you are in this Message of the Hour, which is nothing but Jesus Christ, don't look back, don't look sideways, move ahead! And possess your ground. There is no spirit which does not know that Jesus Christ is the conqueror. Yeah, every spirit knows because He conquered those spirits there at Calvary. And He has given us His name, His blood. That's why we have to know even the value of the cross of Jesus. We have to know the purpose of the cross of Christ.

[44] So, brothers and sisters, because of time, may God bless you. Let us pray. Gracious eternal heavenly Father, in the name of Jesus Christ, we want to thank you Lord for this evening. We want to thank you Father that you have spoken unto us, O Father, in a simple way, and that is your manner of your talking. What you have given us Lord, may you keep it by the Holy Ghost. May it fall into a good ground that it may germinate and bear fruits, for your glory and for our edification. Bless your children, bless the pastor, bless all the ministers, bless us all mighty God, in the name of Jesus Christ we pray, amen. God bless you.

# Wondrous things in God's Word

[1] Psalms 119:18. Let's pray. Most gracious Father, in the name of Jesus Christ, we want to thank you Lord for the testimony which has gone forth. We have seen the fruits of that testimony, and here again Father we are calling upon you, excellent one, to come and take over the preaching of the Word. As we read the Word give us blessings Father. Speak to us the Bread of Life. We are seated at your table. Make us to eat and drink at your table Father. Open our eyes, open our ears, open our hearts Father, for we are here to hear. In the name of Jesus Christ we pray. Amen.

[2] Before you sit let us read this verse, Psalm 119:18 [Pastor Mawino urges people to stand]:

*Open thou mine eyes, that I may behold wondrous things out of thy law.*

May the Lord bless His Word. You can be seated.

[3] The Lord bless you richly. We are now going to share the Word. So this was a prayer of a man called David. You know David was a spiritual man. He was a man who had fought so many wars. He had seen the power of the living God and he knew how God could deliver him. But he is making a very special prayer here. He says, "Lord open my eyes so that I can see wondrous things out of thy word." We want to entitle our sharing, "Wondrous things which are in God's Word".

⁴ This Bible here is carrying wondrous things! And all those wondrous things are yours. All those wondrous things are mine. But we need our eyes to be opened to see these wondrous things because they are there for us. What are those wondrous things? We are going to pull them one by one as the Lord will lead us. One of those wondrous things, which are in the Word of God, is the Power of God.

⁵ The Power of God is the *grace* of God, and this power is yours. It is put there for you. And you need your eyes to be opened so that you can utilize this power. So that you can use this power, so that you speak this power, so that this power becomes your property, so that this power becomes your inheritance. That is one of the things we want to pull out. Because if you can get that power then you are going to live this life very happy.

⁶ Many Christians are living a miserable life because they have not seen this power of God; they don't know that this power belongs to them. And because they don't know they are living a life of trembling. They are living a life of fear. They are living a life of bondage. Why? They don't see this power, but it is there in the Word of God! And it is yours, you need just to open your eyes. When God opens your eyes then you can see, then you can possess, then you can use, then you can inherit,

because it is yours! Wondrous things out of God's Word. And we are going to see them.

[7] My life on earth is just to enjoy this power. I remember when I use to stay in Teso. The Karamojong use to come and raid Teso. And *in* those days they had guns. And the way they shoot, the gun they shoot, its sound is completely different. The sound of the gun is *taaa---tooo, taaa---tooo* [congregation laughs Ed]. When you hear that if you have strength you flee, run! Because they are just going to catch you. So one time they came and I was in the garden of Cassava, early in the morning, I heard a gun *taa---tooo* [congregation laughs]. So I knew they were the ones. I ran from the garden. Reaching home the sister was trying to carry the children, big people were running. So I ran from my home with my bicycle with two children. Running in the middle of the bush, the sound of guns was coming closer and closer. I threw the bike off. I took off the children. All of us went up to Soroti. Now the army men could come but those people don't know the… As long as they have a gun…is nothing…

[8] In the evening as we came back after they had gone, I looked where I had put the bicycle I found the bicycle was not there. I said, "Thank you Jesus! This is the bicycle which a brother gave me for the work of God, now God has given it to somebody. I

don't know who is that person, God thank you, but all the same you are a restorer". So I continued home.

$^9$ As I sat at my place [home], late in the evening, I saw a man coming with a bicycle. The behind [rear] wheel was locked. So he was only using the *front* wheel. He had lifted it from behind, rolling it. I saw him coming. The road was just in front of the house. So when he reached there I greeted him. I saw that the bicycle was mine. I said, "Hey, how are you my friend?"

"I am fine. You know this bicycle; I misplaced the key because the Karamojong were chasing us. Now I don't know where I put the key".

I said, "Oh sorry, sorry."

Of course I had the key. So I went there, I said, "Just wait, Just wait".

I got the key, I opened the bicycle…[Inaudible. People in audience clap ]...So, that's the power I am talking about! The power is in the Word of God!

$^{10}$ David said, "Open my eyes that I may see wondrous things". One of those things is the power! It is hiding there in the word of God. It is yours. Any time your eyes are opened you are not going to fear because this power is your only protection, it is your only confidence. And the power of God has everything.

$^{11}$ What made Meshack, Shadrach and Abednego

stand in the fire? It was the power of God which was in the Word of God ...Wondrous things in the Word of God and one of them is the power.

[12] You know this power, it is so simple. One time as I was walking on the road to go and preach I saw great rain *coming* in front of me. I told God, "Oh, thank you God! You are the creator of everything, *including this rain here*. Now this rain here, I don't want to wet my Bible. I want this rain to go this side, and as I reach where it is, I want it left on my back, no rain, Lord push the rain!"

[13] He [God] brought a wind from the north side, I mean from south. It pushed the rain, very strong wind! The water only came from where I am, the rain has already passed. I was dry.

[14] I continued walking to the place I was going to preach. When I reached there, after preaching, I went to another person. Those were the days of Idi Amin. While I was still in Teso, I was not even married, then I was arrested by the police. Because Amin had not allowed preaching in his days. I was arrested by the police. They put the chain on my hands. They took me to the police cell. So, when I entered there I found a group of thieves, criminals! So they removed the chains and said, "You sit there, among your friends". I sat there, then I stood up. I began preaching...

[15] As I was preaching those people believed. They

knelt down and I was praying for them. Then the policeman came in. "You man, what are you doing there?"

I said, "Sir, I am preaching".

"Who are you?" He asked.

I said, "I am a Karamojong. I used to be a thief, I used to be a killer, Jesus has saved me, and now I am preaching."

The man looked at me. I told him, "If it is forbidden to preach...If you don't want me to preach give me a license, I am going to steal, I am going to kill, I begin with police" [congregation laughs and claps].

They asked, "Where are you from?"

I said, "I am ... from Karamoja region"

They said, "go..go..go... get out of this place!"

[16] The power is in the Word of God. I have seen even ... sisters in Karamoja. One sister was bitten by a snake in the garden. The place was around the lake. She looked...said, "There is nothing here, no poison at all, I am a child of God"... A poisonous snake, a snake which can kill you! The sister said, "There is nothing here! Jesus took the poison!" So she continued doing her work.

[17] One sister, she had gone to the well to get water. One neighbour poisoned her child, put the poison in the food. When she came, the sister found the child died...She took the child inside the house

and prayed for the child. The child was healed! In the evening, by 7 in the night, the other woman came crawling, she was so sick dying. She came crawling pleading, "I am dying, it was me who poisoned the child. Please forgive me, forgive me"... The sister said, "May God forgive you, go back home", she stood up and she went.

[18] Wondrous things out of God's Word! But do you know that these things are yours? Do you know that these powers are yours?

[19] It takes the revelation for you to know, for you to perceive. Your eyes must be opened. Remember God was asking the church of Laodicea, He said, "I come for you, that you come and buy the medicine of your eyes so that you can see".[41] You need to get the medicine so that your eyes are open, that you may know that power in the Word of God. It is there in the Scriptures and it is yours. It is idle there, and it is you to use it. This power.

[20] Who made the lions not to eat Daniel? It was the power of God which is in the Word. What made Paul and Silas to come out of prison? It was the power of God. What made Peter to come out of prison? It was the power of God. There are wondrous things in the Word, and those are things we need to enjoy.

[21] Now, here, let's see another thing. There in the

---

[41] Rev.3:18.

Word of God there is a true marriage. It is there! Those are wondrous things in the Word. One of them is marriage. You need to know, you younger brother, you younger sister, you need to know your husband is in the Word. Your wife, she is in the Word. You need just your eyes to be opened so that you can see her, so that you can see him. He is there. Wondrous things out of the Word.

[22] That is why Abraham told Eleazar, "I want you to go to my relatives, go and bring a wife for my son, I don't want women of this land..." That is in Genesis 24. Now, Eleazar was a very spiritual man. He knew the wife was in the Word. When he moved away he prayed. He said, "Lord, have respect to the prayer of my father Abraham. My master is sending me, I am also praying, as I go I will come to a place where comes men to drink water. Now, I am going to pray like this: that the girl, the first girl I meet I will tell her, 'Give me water to drink', and if she can say, 'I will give you *and your animals to drink'*. Let that one be the wife of Isaac". Wondrous things out of God's Word. Rebecca was there in the Word of God. So Eleazar used the Word for Rebecca to appear.

[23] So, as he went, the first lady he saw was Rebecca. He went near her, greeted her and said, "Please give me water to drink". Then the girl said, "I will give you the water, I will also *give water to*

*the animals.*" The man had to fell down and worship God, because Rebecca has come out of the Word of God. He saw her. But you see, the problem of many Christians, when time for marriage comes, they begin moving from church to church trying to look for a wife. And some move with decision, telling God, "God I want a slender and tall one, educated; she must have finished primary, maybe *Senior 4...*" Some say, "I want a short one and with a body, but at least she should have finished a degree from a university, in the name of Jesus I pray". You are just playing a church game. No, you cannot get a wife or a husband in that manner.

[24] God has got husbands and wives in the Word here, and the only way to get them is to have faith in God, believing that He is responsible for my marriage. Because He was responsible for Adam. He was the one who *told* that it is not good for a man to remain alone, I will give you a *helper...*[42]

[25] God made Adam to sleep, then out of his rib *God made a woman.* So, today why we have problems in families, because the wives we have they are not our ribs. We have ended up marrying somebody's wife ... [congregation laughs]...and so that woman can't fit there, that woman, because she is not yours ... And then you begin running, "Oh, pastor!" ... Because you got someone who was not

---

[42] Gen.2:18.

yours...and now you have hell of her!

[26] You know, the family of a believer is supposed to be a family of happiness and joy. Even though those people know so many things, but the secret we have ... And when believers get their wives according to God, the pastor will have less problems in the church. Because all of them are wives and husbands given by God. And in the word of God they are called sons, they are called daughters, of God.

[27] So God gives His son His daughter, God gives His daughter His son ... and the family becomes heaven and every time there is joy. That's why, some of us who are preachers, when we come back – for me  maybe I am going to be three months outside, I left Uganda in July, and August is ... and I am supposed to go around Tanzania, around Kenya, before I reach home. Maybe I will reach there end of October or the beginning of November. See, you reach there when you are tired. But immediately you reach home, a daughter of God sees a son of God, who is her husband, she comes with open heart. But you see, how many sisters who cannot even embrace their husbands? [Noisy responses from congregants - Ed]...Why don't you embrace him? ...

[28] Wondrous things out of God's Word. Those women, those men, are wondrous. They are from

God's Word. Because God will not give you something which is not ... He gave Adam a suitable one. A suitable one! Let me tell you, I got married in 1977, and from that year up to today my wife has never lost her beauty. She is still so beautiful as the first time ... [Congregation applauds]. She is still very very beautiful because she came out of God's Word. And everything which is a product of God's Word is beautiful. The husband who comes by God's Word is beautiful. And the love, it never grows old ... Why? Because both of you came from God. You are the children of the Word and every day the Word of God lives in you ...

[29] Yeah, wondrous things out of the Word. They are there. And we need to realise that the Word of God is hiding so many things for us...

[30] You see the children of Israel came out of Egypt by God's power, with the power of God ... Now, that power is still existing up to today. That is why you see the Karamojong who used to kill ... people, immediately the Word was given the power of God went inside them and they were transformed, they were changed and they became suitable vessels of God! Those are the things we desire.

[31] Another thing which came out of God's Word is the Holy Ghost. The Holy Ghost is there in the Word. Because, those who receive the Holy Ghost

are people who believe the Word! And the *Holy Ghost* comes from the Word. He comes from the Word.

[32] That's why Paul was telling them, "Have you received the Holy Ghost since you believed?" They said, "We don't know...". "How were you baptised, you do not have the Holy Ghost?"[43] Because the Holy Ghost He is with the Word. Provided you have believed the Word, as long as you have believed the Word, the Holy Ghost has to come. Yeah, because the Holy Ghost comes upon the believers of the Word.

[33] Those are wondrous things. The Holy Ghost is a wondrous thing! And it is *for* you and me to get it, because Jesus said it will make you my witness, from Jerusalem, all of Judea, Samaria, and the end of the world. It is there in the Word. If you don't have it, tell God, "God I have believed the Word but now fill me with the Holy Ghost", and God will do it!

[34] One time there were brothers who wanted to be baptised, to receive the Holy Spirit, and they had decided, "Let us go to Brother John Mark to pray for us to receive the Holy Spirit". Now, John Mark is a sojourner; if you want to chase for me you have to have a good shoes for moving, otherwise you are in trouble. So they followed me. They reached

---

[43] Act.19:1-5.

somewhere, a certain home. *They were told,* "Oh John Mark was here but he has left for such and such a place". Then they reached somewhere. "Oh, he was here but ... he has left for such and such a place." Now, they just decided that, "He slept here, let's also sleep here, let's call on God and let Him give us the Holy Ghost. We are not going to follow him. God is with us, we have the Word, we have believed the Word, why are we *looking for John Mark.* Let's call on God to give us the Holy Ghost!". *They* knelt down, they sung, they prayed ... All of them were filled with the Holy Ghost. They went back rejoicing, because they got the Holy Ghost.

[35] So, there are wondrous things out of the Word. What are those things? Let's pull out the messages, from end to end. Because when you see the Bible you will see the promises and those promises are the ones which you can see the messages of *ages.* Now, in our age it is written that I will send you Elijah the prophet. *Where is that?* It's in the Word! That is one of the wonders! That is one of the mighty things of God – the message of the age!

[36] Now, it is only those who are predestinated, whose names are written in the Lamb's Book of Life, they are the ones who can see the Message of the Hour in the Bible. And they will enjoy it and *take it* as their own property; it becomes your own

possession.

[37] The Message of the Hour, it is there in the Word. But it is you now and me who can see it and pull it out and use it and possess it. You know, it is ours! But it is in the Word. But the Pentecostal will say, "Where is Elijah? Where is the Message of the Hour? You people are liars! We don't see it! We have seen Malachi, it doesn't talk about Branham! Where is your Message? Where is your messenger?"[44] They cannot see it because their eyes are not opened. But you, who is an elect, your eyes have been opened, your ears have been opened, God has opened, to receive the Message, because it is yours but it's from the Word.

[38] Healing is one of the wondrous things in the Word of God. It is there. *For* every disease, the medicine is in the Word. Now, there was a great *man called* Naaman in the land of Syria.[45] He was a mighty man. He was a mighty army-man but he was a leper. Then there was a girl who was abducted from Israel by the army of Syria. She was in the house of Naaman. So, she looked at the man. He had no fingers in the hands and *no toes* in the legs, but he was a big man. The army men would come and they salute him but the man has no ... This little girl was so touched. She said, "I wish this

---

[44] Mal.4:5-6.
[45] 2 Kin.5:1-14.

man could go to Israel and meet the prophet of God, he will get healed". *Then the girl talked to the wife of the man.* She said, "Mama, if your husband goes to Israel that leprosy, it will disappear … Because there is a prophet in the land of Israel, he has been used of God..." So the message went up to the king.

[39] The king said, "Okay, let's write a letter to the king of Israel" and the letter was sent. When the king read *it*, he was afraid. He tore his clothes. When Elisha heard. He said, "Why do you tear your clothes?"... Then the man was sent. Elisha told him ... Elisha sent the messenger to the king ... "Go and tell Naaman, you go and deep thyself seven times in Jordan. On the seventh round your body will look like of a baby". Now, this man was very angry. He said, "Ahhh, this prophet! I know he could come, welcome me, I am a big man ... I am *an* honourable man. I thought he would come and then greet me and then touch-touch my body in the name of his god and I get recovered. He is telling me to go to River Jordan! Why can't he send me to *one of the rivers* in Syria and Damascus? ... Jordan? Ah, I can't go there!"

[40] He was rejecting the healing which came from the Word of God by human reasoning. Then his bodyguard *told him,* "If a prophet has told you a hard thing I believe you would have done it, what

about now this *simple* thing? Can't you do it? ... Why can't you just go *and deep yourself in the river?"*

[41] Where did the prophet *get* that? From the Word. Those are wondrous things, but they are hidden there. But it is you, who is an elect, who has eyes, who has a heart to believe, you are the one who can possess that, because it is yours.

[42] So the man went and dipped himself in the river. On the seventh round he came out clean. Why? Because healing is from the Word. It is there in the Word.

[43] Now, let's talk about spiritual resurrection. According to John 5:24-25, Ephesians 2:1. In John Jesus said:

*Verily, verily, I say unto you, He that heareth my word, and believeth on him that sent me, hath everlasting life, and shall not come into condemnation, but is passed from death unto life.*

*Verily, verily, I say unto you, the hour is coming, and now is, when the dead shall hear the voice of the Son of God: and they that hear shall live.*

Paul said, in Ephesians, "You who had died in your sins and trespasses, by faith God has quickened you!"[46] What is that? Spiritual resurrection! A resurrection of the soul, which had been killed by sin. Because when sin came in the

---

[46] Eph.2:5.

Garden of Eden, it *was* through the spirit of man. It killed Adam, it killed his wife, and since all of us were in the loins of Adam, all of us were killed, because we were there in Adam. So that when all of us were born, we were born as dead people because of the sin in the garden.

[44] But Jesus said, "Those dead ones, the time has come for them to hear the voice of the son of God, so that they come to life".[47] Spiritual resurrection, from the Word of God! ... That's why Jesus said, "Go ye into the whole world, preach the Gospel to every creature, he who believes will be baptised and will be saved".[48] Spiritual resurrection from the Word of God. It is hidden there! That is the difference between a true gospel and a perverted gospel!

[45] The gospel of religion is a pervert gospel. You know a religious gospel is like putting milk in a jerrycan of 20 litres, and then you get a drum of 500 litres, you fill water there, then you pour this milk here into that 500 litres, then you call it milk. It is so tasteless, the colour has changed, the colour is no longer white, but it is grey. Why? Because it is so much watered until the milk has lost its colour. *It is the same as* drinking tea, hot water, without milk. So, that is a gospel of religion! That is why

---

[47] Joh.5:25.
[48] Mar.16:15-16.

religion cannot resurrect the souls of human beings. They cannot resurrect!

[46] That is why the people who are in religion are still dead as they were. Because the gospel they are given is a hybrid watered gospel. Just what we can call entertainment gospel. They just go there, with their instruments, and then they begin singing ... singing, calling people to come, no preaching at all ... and then they say they are saved. The Word has not resurrected them. They are still dead in sin. It is the true gospel that can resurrect them.

47 Yes, let's pull another one. The New Birth. Those are wondrous things in the Word. The new birth is in the Word of God. When you hear the true gospel you are born again. Now, to me "born again" means that you have heard the Word, accepted and you are begotten by the Word. And when you now come to the church, you came to the church as somebody who is born again.

[48] Now, you begin to bring out the characteristics of God. Love, you are not told about it. It's the nature of your Father and you are born by Him. That is why the Bible says, "As for loving a brother, you don't need anybody to teach you".[49] You are born with it! ... You are born with it! The new birth, it is in the Word of God. What you only need is for God to send ordained true ministers,

---

[49] 1 The.4:9.

who are going to bring this Gospel to all the sinners and this Gospel is looking for the true seed.

[49] He comes to look for the seed, the true seed. And if you are the true seed, who was predestinated for life before the foundation of the world, the Gospel is going to find its way into your soul. It is going to go deep into your soul, bring resurrection, bring a new birth, from there you become a baby in God's house. That is why Peter said, "As a new born baby you desire the sincere milk of the Gospel whereby you grow into Salvation".[50] Yeah, because ...

[50] Now, this new birth here has given you the life of God. How do you know this? By the Word of God. Because it's the Word of God, there ... which has been preached, when the true seeds hear, they are born again. Then they begin to grow. As they are beginning to hear the Word. Of course "growth", we are told in Genesis 17, when Abraham was 99 years, God met him. He said, "I am Elshaddai, the Almighty God, I am the one who has given you *new life,* you are born again by me, and I am Elshaddai, I am the breast. You walk before me, suck me and you will live".[51]

[51] Now, that is what we call growth. That's why Peter said, "New babies desire the milk of the

---

[50] 1 Pet.2:2.
[51] Gen.17:1.

Gospel which gives them the growth into Salvation".[52] Wondrous things out of God's Word, a new birth.

[52] Then when you are born again you are never the same. That's why, you see, the Bible has testimonies of those who are born again. Some of them were harlots, thieves, murderers, liars, those like Jacob. But a new birth made a difference. It changed a man like Jacob. He was no longer Jacob, he was Israel, a prince of God, because a new birth has taken place. And when a church, all the church members are born again, then they can now grow, from one degree to another, from faith to faith.

[53] Because in the body there are five offices, and all these offices, they are the breast of God for the bride. Your duty is to suck the breast of God of apostles, you suck the prophets, you suck the evangelists, you suck the pastors, and teachers, for the perfection of the body. Yes, a new birth. A new birth comes by the Word.

[54] It is the Word who is hiding there. The Word is hiding. And now, as long as you are a seed, you are going to find yourself  enjoying all those things. Yes. Then we can name them in number.

[55] Now, after you have grown, you are filled with the Holy Ghost, and you have walked faithfully, then now the Holy Ghost has to endorse your

---

[52] 1 Pet.2:2.

growth; that you have accepted, you have sucked the breast, you have grown, and you are now mature; walking with the Holy Ghost, sucking from the Holy Ghost, and the Holy Ghost now becomes happy, then he endorses your Christianity with the fruits of the Holy Spirit.

[56] Yeah, He now gives you the fruits. Now, these fruits now here, is only given to the mature. And all those who have the fruits, Matthews 13:8, Jesus said *that* some fruits were thirty, some sixty, some hundred. Now, all of them are all the fruits of the Holy Spirit. Paul talks about them in the book of Galatians 5:22-23. He talks about the fruits. Jesus talks *about them* in John 15:8, He said, "By this will my Father be glorified, if you can go and bear much fruit you will be my disciples indeed". The fruits of the Holy Spirit.

[57] Now, the fruits of the Holy Spirit, is, it looks like a reward *given to you* by the Holy Spirit because of your *responsiveness* ... The Holy Ghost now gives you a reward as a sign that you have walked with Him, you have obeyed Him, and now the fruit is given.

[58] Let us pull another one called victorious Christian living. It's from the Word. A victorious life comes from the Word. A victorious life comes from the Word! Because when you are enjoying the Word and believe it and use it, you are living a

victorious life.

[59] Now, in the area of this victorious life, there is now a reward. That's why, people like those of Daniel, all those of .., all those of Joshua, they were rewarded with certain things of the Word ... Now, Jesus said, Revelation 3:21, "Him who overcomes, he will sit with me in my throne as I overcame and sat with my Father in His throne". Now, that is *a word to overcomers.*

[60] What are you to overcome? There are three enemies you have to overcome. Remember we are talking about "Wondrous things out of the Word". Victorious Christian living. Now, Jesus said, "him that overcomes will sit with me in my throne as I did overcome, I sat with my Father in His throne". Now, what have you overcome? Because you cannot be given a reward unless you have overcome! There are many Christians who say, "Pastor, you know, I was alone in my church, there was no church, so because of that my Christianity *became* weak, and therefore I *fell*". But, how are you going to get a reward if you are just falling? How are you going to get a reward? You are supposed to live a victorious life by the power of the Word of God.

[61] Paul said, "The weapons of our fighting are not *weak,* they are not of the flesh; they are mighty,

because they are from God".[53] That is, from the Word. Yeah, we are supposed to overcome all enemies by the power of the Word of God! At least there are three, leave the rest. Let's just bring out the three, our time is running. One of them is the flesh.

[62] The flesh is the nearest enemy to every Christian. And if you are not going to overcome the flesh you are in trouble. Remember the flesh is the workshop of the Devil. So, you need to overcome the flesh by using the providence of God. Telling the flesh, if the flesh says, "Oh, now, you younger man, in your church *there are* only old women, there is no girl, now you have grown up, where are you going to get a wife? You just come around, around a bar here, there are beautiful girls here, pick one and then you go back to your ..." Tell the flesh, "It is written that God is the one who can give a wife, because He gave Adam, because He gave Isaac, and the whole Bible is full of men who *got* wives from God, the wives had husbands from God ... Flesh be subject to the Word, you rest until God's time for you to have a wife!" Yes, you have to command the flesh.

[63] Because it is the flesh which leads many people to sin. Even this work of paying tithe or offering. The flesh, if you have got money, maybe of about

---

[53] 2 Cor.10:4.

five million, it will tell you, "Ahh, now, this five million, it is now five hundred tithe for the church, but now you postpone that, you transfer this money because you have problems in the house, school fees ... use that money..." That is the flesh, and if you accept the flesh then you have transgressed the law of God because the flesh now will keep postponing everything.

[64] So, the flesh and the world. The world is also another great enemy you have to overcome. 1 John 2:15, "Love not the world, neither the things which are in the world. If anyone loves the world the love of the Father is not in him. Because all that is in the world: it is the lust of eyes, it is the pride of life, and it is the lust of the flesh, and all those things do not come from God. They are from the world. The world will pass away, and all those things; he who does the will of God remains forever". You need to overcome the world; the flesh and the world.

[65] Then comes Satan! At least those three enemies, they are the ones we have to overcome by living a life of principle, a life of *transformation, a* life of holiness.

[66] Now, after we have overcome the three, then there is a reward, and the reward is in three ways. One part of the reward is the rapture. Another part of the reward is having crowns with the Lord, there in the Marriage Supper. The third part of the reward

is ruling with Christ.

[67] So, you cannot have those things – the rapture, a crown, *and* ruling with Christ for *a* thousand years - if you have not overcome. Because Jesus said "after you have *overcome* you will now sit with me, in my throne".[54] Meaning that you will be with Him in *the* Millennium, ruling with Him for a thousand years. Wondrous things out of God's Word. So, I want us think seriously on those things.

[68] So, since our time is running out, I want to encourage you that, there are many things in the Word of God, even children. Some people after marrying, they can stay for three to five years ... *You say,* "This sister is not fruitful! No child...*but* she is very young". Then you begin to look for a witch doctor. But children are in the Word! God, He has power to give you children! ... There are many, many other things which are here in the Word of God.

[69] One of them is what we call daily fellowship. We get this from the Word. Fellowshipping with God, with one another. We get all those things from the Word. So, let's focus our eyes on the Word and ask God to open our eyes that we may see those things, and then possess them, use them, for our redemption.

[70] As long as we can use them then we ... The

---

[54] Rev.3:21.

Word of God is like a lorry *which* is loaded with commodities: sacks of millet, sacks of maize, sugar, litres of oil. Now, this is the lorry of our desire, its work is to serve. So, when it comes to the town, every shop keeper goes to this lorry with his or her money to buy the commodities and put in their shops. Until the lorry is completely empty he goes again to take some more. So, in this church, this Word here is put into the hands of the pastor and ministers. The revelations which are here, powers which are here,  God put it there so that they can impart unto the church. When they are over he goes to get another one, he gives, when they are over, he goes to get another and gives. Because it is written, in Jeremiah 3:15, God says, "I will give you pastors according to my heart, who will give you knowledge and understanding".

[71] So it is my prayer that God gives us grace to see these wondrous things in the Word of God. Let me say, the Lord bless you. I want to thank you all. I want to thank the pastor, the ministers and deacons, how we have been together for these few moments … As for me I really say that I am at home, because I am not a visitor here, it is my home, you are my brothers and sisters. And when I am here I will be at home. So, it is my prayer that God *blesses* you.

# Farewell
*It was his final "Round"*

From Zambia Brother John Mark was scheduled to visit Zimbabwe. From Zimbabwe he was to come back to Zambia and then move on to Kenya.

One day whilst having our breakfast meal on a table in the sitting room of our home we were talking about his itinerary, and how it would be good for him to visit many other places again. Smilingly he said, "You know, the Lord had spoken to me about this before I came here. He told me that he would raise someone for me to have another round of moving to different places to preach." After saying this, he exclaimed, "But after all the things I have seen in my ministry, I wonder what great things will happen again!"

My thoughts went back to some months earlier when I was driving home with my wife and I suddenly interrupted a conversation we were having, saying, "Lets arrange for Brother John Mark to come, Won't it be wonderful?"

I informed brothers and sisters at Believers Assembly of the thought and everyone seemed in support of it. We then started making savings of the money required for his transport costs from Uganda to Zambia. Well, the rest is history. He visited Zambia and ministered in different congregations.

Shortly after Brother John Mark had returned to

his home in Karamoja - after a round of many missionary trips to places he had never been for quite a long time - I phoned him. His voice sounded frail and I wondered why he sounded like that. He spoke very slowly. Later on I was informed by his eldest son that he was critically ill. Shortly around that time I had my missionary trip to Asia. Whilst in Singapore I received the news that Brother John Mark was showing signs of recovery. With Brother Richard Gan we were glad and hopeful of his full recovery. However, shortly after my return home I received the news that Brother John Mark had gone to be with the Lord. He died on 26th February 2015. The news shook our souls! It was just so unexpected. About a week after that, our fellowship received a comforting word from the Lord through Brother Annel Silungwe, a congregant at Believers' Assembly.

## Dream by Brother Annel Silungwe

In my dream, to this day, I remember so vividly the sentence *"Do not worry about the passing of Brother John Mark"* like it happened yesterday. After much interaction and travelling to the southern province of Zambia in Choma, with Pastor John Mark, where we stayed for one week I was personally inspired by his humility. Many times at our lodge Pastor John Mark and I shared moments especially when he spoke of very simple but yet powerful testimony of how he recovered his stolen bicycle and money on a bus. Some years before I had read his testimony of how he was called into the ministry and I was very much privileged to have accompanied him on this trip.

When the pastor was finally back home in Uganda I phoned him to just check on him and find out if he travelled safely but he sounded so low that I thought he had not recognized me. I said, "It's me brother…" in trying to introduce myself to him but he responded saying, "I know brother". We spoke for a short time and the network connection got cut.

I kept wondering what was wrong until the day I received the news of his passing. I was confused, heart-broken and I kept asking "Why Lord have you permitted this to happen? A gallant servant, an anointed man to die?" It was unbelievable. A thought struck and I remembered that he had run and fought his fight well.

The following year, between January and February of 2015, I had a very strange and short dream in which I was crying and mourning still asking the Lord as to why he had taken Brother John Mark. It was at a gathering of many believers who were equally all heartbroken because we all, including Brother John Mark himself believed that he was going to have a second round of preaching in southern Africa.

Suddenly a voice came and said "*Do not worry about the passing of Brother John Mark*". I woke up and found tears still running down my face. I was literally crying. I testified of this incidence during the main Sunday service at Believers' Assembly. Brother John Mark had his final round. (*End of testimony by Bro. Annel Silungwe*).

The messages Brother John Mark preached admonished believers to stand on the Word and to have faith. More importantly to note is that before his journey he had a strange dream of seeing ministers naked. He was distressed by the dream as he wondered, "Why are these ministers naked?" The Lord answered him that the nakedness meant the lack of the Holy Spirit in many men who are professing to preach. In this round of missionary trips to various places in Zambia, Zimbabwe and Kenya, this apostle of faith bid farewell without knowing that his ministry had run its course.

Andrew  C. Phiri
*Zambia*

## *Epilogue & Testimony of Brother Richard Gan*

*Presented at the funeral service of John Mark*

To the family of my dear brother, John Mark Louse, my condolences for your loss of a husband and father, and to the saints of his assembly, my pain for the loss of a pastor whom you so dearly loved. To all fellow saints, who are of the household of God and of our Lord and Saviour Jesus Christ, who are assembled here today to mourn the passing of a mighty man of God, please accept my absence.

I greet all in the wonderful name of our Lord and Saviour Jesus Christ. Needless to say, our hearts are filled with grief and some heaviness as to "why" Brother John Mark is no longer with us; a servant of God who still had much to give to the saints and people in Uganda, and even the nations surrounding its border. The word "why", is in our heart whenever someone precious and dear to us is taken away from us. The "why" question, is then posted to our God, our Heavenly Father – "Why, Lord, did you have to take my husband?" "Why, Lord, did you have to take away my father?" "Why, Lord, did you have to take away our pastor?" "Why, Lord, did you have to take away this wonderful humble servant from visiting us ever again?" Why, oh why?

But this one thing we all know: that life is like a vapour that appears for a little while and then it vanishes away. The Lord giveth and the Lord taketh away. If that be so, then it matters not how long we live, rather it is how well we live this life. Consider our Lord and Saviour, Jesus Christ. His life was short, cut off in His prime, at the age of thirty-three and a half years old. But in that short span of life, He had influenced the world forever. Our dear brother, John Mark Louse, had nearly twice the lifespan of our Lord. And he too had influenced many lives forever. He will never be forgotten for the good that he had left behind. Truly, he had lived well.

Let me tell you how Brother John Mark and I got acquainted. It was during my second visit to Uganda. (I kept no record of the year but I believe my first visit was in 1993. I am unable to remember when the second visit was; perhaps it was 2 years after). I was to go to Kasese and had requested Pastor Peter Ochola, in advance, to have Brother John Mark come down to Kampala to accompany me to Kasese. While we were together, Brother John Mark told me about what happened in my first visit. He told me what was on his mind when he was informed to meet me in Soroti for the meeting. He said that he was not going because he had had enough of foreign End Time Message preachers and he considered me to be one of those preachers that had foolish understanding of the prophet's message. However, he said his wife told him, "You should not judge the man until you have heard him." Realizing the wisdom of his wife, he decided to go and was carefully observing that first message I delivered; "The Bottomless Pit". He was excited and told Pastor Peter Ochola, "I can identify with this man."

In Kasese, on the second day, Brother John Mark had an open vision. We were up early in the morning and ventured out of the hotel to sit on a hill nearby which overlooked a valley with the sun rising from behind the distant hills. It was beautiful. We sat there and opened our mouths, worshipping and praying. After about 20 minutes Brother John Mark stopped. I stopped after a little while. I turned and asked him why he stopped as we were in the presence of the Lord. He said, "Because I saw something wonderful and I wanted to tell you." When asked what he saw, he said, "I saw a vision of you and Jesus Christ standing on a platform. And both of you were facing each other. The Lord then said this to you: "My servant, be steadfast and teach what I have given you, wherever I send you. Do not be afraid to speak that which I have put in your mouth. Be strong in the faith..."

There was more than what I can remember of what Brother John Mark saw and heard in the vision. But the vision was to me a reinforcement of what was spoken to me in 1984 in Brother Raymond Jackson's church, in Jeffersonville, Indiana, USA. The vision shown to Brother John Mark was important to me, but what was more important was how God got the both of us together for the ministry there in Uganda and the surrounding nations. It was in these two visits that we both bonded. I saw in Brother John Mark Louse, something unique, a gifted man, a simple man. And he saw in me who I was in the ministry of the Lord. There were many things we shared and talked about. I was blessed by his testimony of how he was called to the ministry. We have so much in common, most of all, the Truth of the End Time Message and the revelation of our Lord Jesus Christ.

A gallant soldier of the Lord, a mighty warrior of Christ was our Brother John Mark Louse. I can never forget the brother, and likewise, the many saints whose lives were influenced by this man of God. And so, if only Brother John Mark could hear me, I would say this: "Have a good night of rest, my dear John Mark. Rest my brother, my friend, sleep well. We will see you in the morning, just inside that Eastern Gate." Amen.

Richard Gan
*Singapore*

www.ingramcontent.com/pod-product-compliance
Lightning Source LLC
Chambersburg PA
CBHW071524150726
48000CB00002B/674